FORTNITE BATTLE ROYALE HACKS

ADVANCED STRATEGIES

FORTNITE BATTLE ROYALE HACKS

ADVANCED STRATEGIES

THE UNOFFICAL GUIDE TO TIPS AND TRICKS THAT OTHER GUIDES WON'T TEACH YOU

JASON R. RICH

SKY PONY PRESS

Sky Pony Press
New York

Sky Pony Press books may be purchased in bulk at special discounts for sales promotion, corporate gifts, fund-raising, or educational purposes. Special editions can also be created to specifications. For details, contact the Special Sales Department, Sky Pony Press, 307 West 36th Street, 11th Floor, New York, NY 10018 or info@skyhorsepublishing.com.

Sky Pony® is a registered trademark of Skyhorse Publishing, Inc.®, a Delaware corporation.

Visit our website at www.skyponypress.com.

Authors, books, and more at SkyPonyPressBlog.com.

10 9 8 7 6 5 4 3 2 1

Library of Congress Cataloging-in-Publication Data is available on file.

Cover design by Brian Peterson

Print ISBN: 978-1-5107-4190-4
E-Book ISBN: 978-1-5107-4191-1

Printed in the United States of America

TABLE OF CONTENTS

SECTION 1

WELCOME TO THE ISLAND: DISCOVER WHAT'S NEW

Ask any gamer what the most popular game in the world is right now, and chances are, they'll tell you it's **Fortnite: Battle Royale**!

In addition to offering exciting and challenging gameplay, this game allows players to compete in real-time against up to 99 others during each exciting and action-packed match.

Game publisher Epic Games has done an amazing job keeping players interested in Fortnite: Battle Royale by continuously introducing new features, gameplay elements, and content. This continuous game evolution makes it even more interesting, fun to play, and increasingly challenging to master.

What You Need to Get Started Playing

Fortnite: Battle Royale is a massively multiplayer online game that's available for Windows PC, Mac, PlayStation 4, Xbox One, iPhone, iPad, and Android-based mobile device. A Nintendo Switch version is rumored to be in development for release in late-2018.

To download the game if you're a PC or Mac computer user, visit www.Fortnite.com (shown above) and click on the yellow Get Fortnite button (found near the bottom-center of the screen). PlayStation 4 users should visit the PlayStation Store, while Xbox One users should visit the Xbox Marketplace.

The iOS mobile device version of the game (shown on the previous page on an iPad Pro) is available from the Apple App Store, while the Android-based version of the game (when it becomes available) can be acquired from the Google Play Store.

A continuous Internet connection is required. If you're playing on a PC or Mac, or any mobile device, you'll also need a free Epic Games account. PlayStation 4 gamers require a PlayStation Network account, while a paid membership to Xbox Gold is required for Xbox One users.

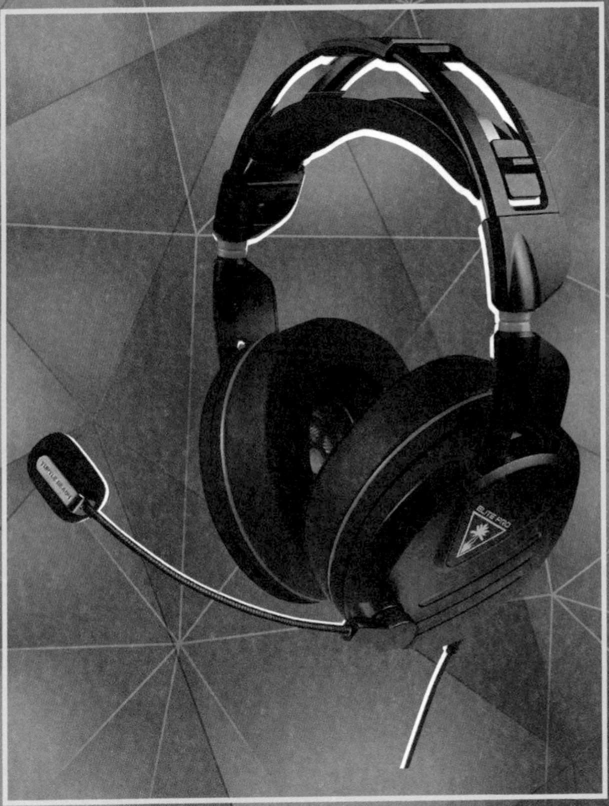

Connecting stereo headphones or a gamer's headset to your gaming system is definitely recommended, since sound is extremely important in this game.

The Cost for Playing Fortnite: Battle Royale

The core Fortnite: Battle Royale game is totally free! For some gaming platforms, however, you can purchase the complete Battle Royale game, which includes story-based "Save the World" missions, but these offer a totally separate gameplay experience from Fortnite: Battle Royale.

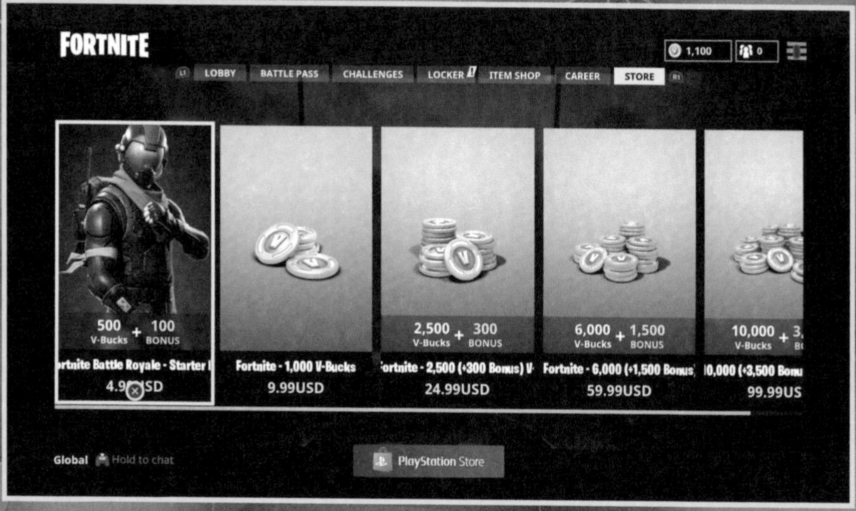

As a Fortnite: Battle Royale player using any gaming platform, you're given the option to purchase V-Bucks (using real money), which can be exchanged for Battle Passes, as well as items from the Item Shop that allow you to customize your character's appearance in the game.

Character customizations have zero impact on a character's fighting ability, speed, strength, aim, or agility within the game. The customizations you make to your character are for appearance purposes only. Many gamers, however, take great pride in creating a fun and unique look for their soldiers.

By completing daily or weekly challenges, completing objectives in Battle Passes, or by redeeming offers from Epic Games's promotional partners, it's possible to acquire customization items for your soldier, and unlock other loot.

If you're an Amazon Prime member and have a Twitch.tv account, periodically free game items are made available for download. These are called Twitch Prime Packs. To learn more, visit www.twitch.tv/prime/fortnite.

Overview of the Game

Almost all of the action in Fortnite: Battle Royale takes place on a mysterious island. The island itself is divided into more than 20 unique points of interest. At the start of each match, you find yourself in the pre-deployment area with many other soldiers. This is where you wait for other players to join the match before it begins.

You and 99 other soldiers are then forced to climb aboard a Battle Bus (a blue bus that flies) to be transported to the island.

Once the bus begins to fly over the island (shown on the previous page), jump out at any time to free fall toward land. You choose when to leap off the bus and where your landing spot will be. As you're in free fall, control the direction your soldier travels. This allows you to traverse more than half the island, if necessary, while in midair.

Each soldier who leaps off the Battle Bus is equipped with a Glider. Once activated, the glider slows your rate of descent and gives you additional navigational control, so you can choose a precise landing spot on the island. During free fall, activate the Glider at any time. However, if you wait too long, the glider activates itself as you get close to land.

Once you set foot on the island, you'll quickly discover that you're stranded there with up to 99 enemy soldiers. You're armed only with a pickaxe (shown on the previous page). Your first two objectives are to find and grab at least one weapon, and to choose a strategy for survival.

The ultimate goal in Fortnite: Battle Royale is survival! Out of the up to 100 soldiers that land on the island during a match, you need to survive and become the last person alive. Sound simple? Well, it's not! Up to 99 other soldiers want to defeat you, and there's a deadly storm to contend with.

Except for the other soldiers on the island, you'll quickly discover that the island is deserted. The buildings (Tilted Towers is shown here), homes, stores, barns, mines, mansions, factories, bases, cars, trucks, towers, and other structures are all empty. What you will find within each point of interest are a selection of weapons, ammo, and loot to collect and use to help your survival efforts. Of course, you'll also likely encounter enemy soldiers who want to end you.

There's also an abundance of resources (wood, stone, and metal) to find and collect throughout the island. These resources are used to build custom walls, structures, ramps, stairs, and fortresses. Use your pickaxe to gather resources.

Resources can also be used at Vending Machines that are scattered throughout the island to purchase rare and powerful weapons or loot.

The Pros and Cons of Fighting

From the moment you land on the island, you could quickly find shelter; try to avoid all enemy soldiers; collect weapons, ammo, and loot; and spend your time exploring the island. However, as a match progresses, if you manage to stay alive, eventually you'll be forced to fight.

Yet another option is to immediately go on the offensive. As soon as you land, grab some weapons, ammo, and loot, and then engage in battle with as many enemy soldiers as you can find. Your experience level in the game will increase with each victory. However, your ultimate goal is to be the last person standing. Even if you're the second-to-last person who remains alive during a match, once you're defeated, it's still game over for you.

Each time you engage in battle with any enemy soldier, there are serious risks. For example, he or she could be more experienced, or be armed with a more diverse and powerful arsenal of weapons. Their HP and Shield meters could be maxed out (meaning they can withstand more damage), or they could be better at quickly building protective walls or fortresses. In addition, every gamer improves their fighting and survival abilities with practice, so your adversary might have faster reflexes, skill, and better aim (when shooting a weapon) than you.

There's Also a Deadly Storm to Contend With

At the same moment you land on the island, a deadly storm begins to form. Don't get caught in the storm for too long, or you'll perish! If you need to escape quickly, and you need to cover a lot of territory in order to reach a safe area of the island, consider using a Launch Pad, if you have one available.

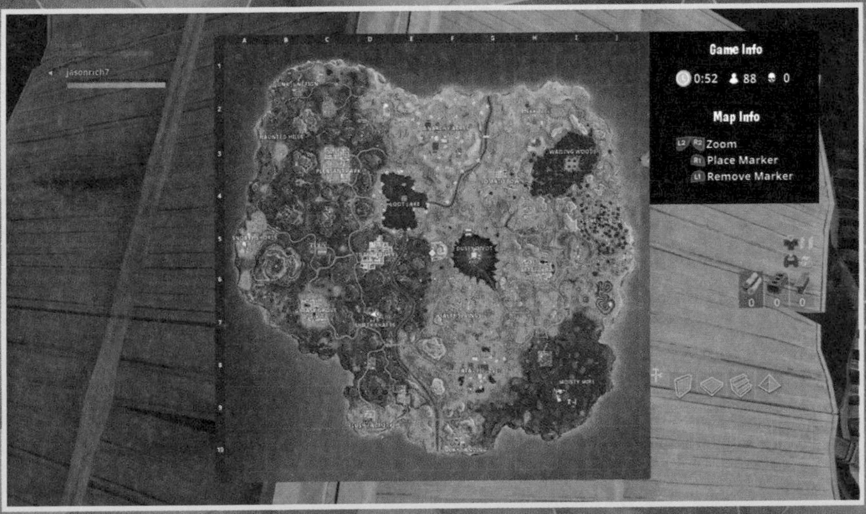

Initially, the entire island is safe and inhabitable. This is what the island map looks like just after you land on the island. However, after a short time, the deadly storm will materialize.

Slowly at first, the deadly storm makes portions of the island uninhabitable. The storm continues to move and expand, until only a small circular area remains safe. If you survive this long, it's within this small circular area where the final battles (known as the End Game) will take place—leaving only one solider alive.

Each time the storm is about to expand and move, you'll hear the sound of a timer ticking, you'll hear and see the storm approaching, and you'll see a warning message appear near the center of the screen.

On the island map, the area of the island that the storm has taken over is displayed in pink. The clear area inside the white circle is the inhabitable (safe) area.

Each match lasts approximately 15 minutes. During this time, the storm will move and expand several times. It's important that you pay careful attention to the storm's progression. Stay in the inhabitable areas of the island (within the circle), as much as possible.

While you can enter the storm for a short time, your HP (Health Points) and Shields will get depleted, slowly at first, but at a faster pace the longer you stay in the storm. You'll also receive more damage when you go inside the storm later in matches.

Walking or even running while stuck inside the storm is a slow process. As the storm moves, if you wind up in a part of the island that's very far from the safe area, you might not be able to escape before your HP and Shields are fully depleted. Your position on the map is displayed as a white triangle icon. If you do get stuck in the storm, follow the white line on the map to safety. It's displayed on the map in the upper-right corner of the screen. (See the previous page.)

Should you find yourself stuck in a storm and you have a Launch Pad in your backpack, build a platform on the ground, place the Launch Pad on top of it, activate it, and then step on it. You'll be catapulted into the air. Your glider will activate, and you'll be able to sail a good distance, hopefully directly toward a safe area. If a Jetpack is available, use it to help you escape the storm quickly.

Fortnite: Battle Royale's GamePlay Modes

In Fortnite: Battle Royale, there are several main gameplay modes. Periodically, additional gameplay modes become available, some for just a limited time. When this happens, a message about it appears in the Lobby prior to a match.

From the Lobby, choose which gameplay mode to experience. Options include: **Solo** (it's you against up to 99 other players), **Duos** (pair up with a friend and defeat up to 98 other soldiers), or **Squads** (invite up to three friends to team up with you, and fight against up to 96 enemy soldiers).

Once you choose Duos or Squads, invite friends to join you from the Lobby. All versions of Fortnite: Battle Royale are cross-platform compatible, so while you may be playing on a Windows PC, for example, you can team up with players using a PS4, an Xbox One, a Mac, or a mobile device.

Experience Seasons in Fortnite

Every two weeks or so, Epic Games releases a game update. This might include new weapons, loot, or challenges. To learn about the latest updates, visit www.epicgames.com/fortnite/en-US/news.

Every few months, however, a new Season of gameplay kicks off. This involves a major game update, which typically includes alternate versions of the island itself, with the introduction of new points of interest and drastic changes to established points of interest. New weapons and loot items are also introduced, along with a selection of themed soldier outfits and accessories. A new Battle Pass also becomes available.

What You Should Know About Battle Passes

At the start of each Season, a new Battle Pass becomes available. For a fee, gamers can purchase an optional Battle Pass, which includes a series of daily and weekly challenges.

In addition to completing daily and weekly challenges, as well as tiers in the current Battle Pass, your character will earn Experience Points (XP) by winning battles and accomplishing other achievements during each match.

Current challenges are displayed on the game's Lobby screen. Here, they're displayed on the left side of the screen, below the character's Level information.

Once you pay for a Battle Pass, from the Lobby, access the Battle Pass screen to discover each tier of challenges that await, and discover what prizes will be unlocked. You can also purchase a Battle Pass from here.

Each time you accomplish one or more of these challenges, new and exclusive loot, character outfits, character accessories, emotes, Experience Point (XP) boosts, unique skydiving trails, spray paint icons, new banner designs, up to 100 V-bucks (which can be used for new loot purchases), or other cosmetic items are unlocked.

Without paying for a Battle Pass, gamers can experience free challenges, but the loot you'll unlock and earn when you complete them is nowhere near as awesome or exclusive. Nothing you unlock by completing challenges offered by a Battle Pass, however, actually improves your soldier's strength, agility, speed, aim, or fighting ability.

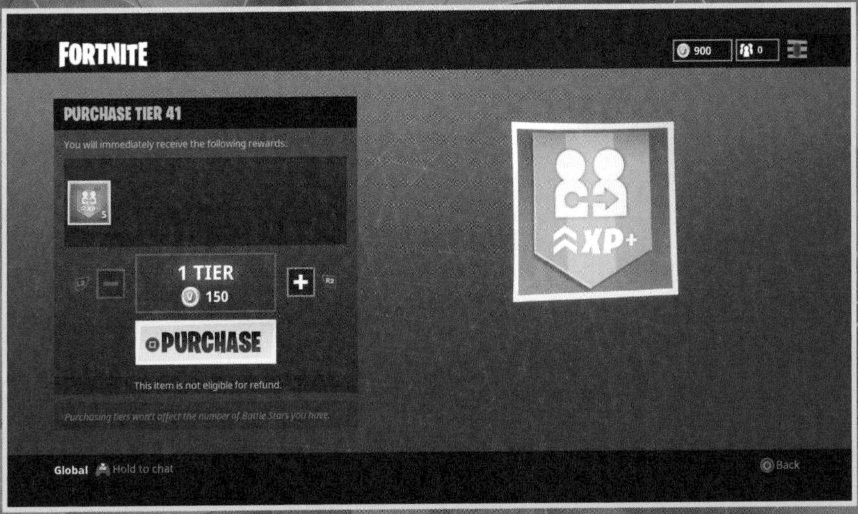

If you want to unlock prizes without actually completing the challenges, purchase (using V-Bucks, which cost real money) the ability to unlock Battle Pass Tiers and collect the loot automatically.

What's New in Fortnite

Since Fortnite: Battle Royale is continuously evolving thanks to game updates from Epic Games, you can expect to see new points of interest on the map, new character outfits, new weapons, as well as new types of loot available to you, beyond what you'll read about in this unofficial strategy guide which was written during Season 4.

During Season 4 (which kicked off in May 2018), the island was pummeled by comets from outer space. Craters began appearing throughout the island. The largest comet destroyed the area formally known as **Dusty Dunes**, and in its place, **Dusty Divot** was build. (Seen on the previous page.)

In addition, new points of interest, including Risky Reels (a drive-in movie theater), were added to the island, along with some awesome new weapons and loot items.

This unofficial strategy guide is chock-full of tips for avoiding the storm, exploring the island, surviving battles against enemy soldiers, and ultimately, winning matches. While knowing these strategies will help you immensely, nothing replaces the need to practice.

The more time you spend actually playing Fortnite: Battle Royale, the easier it will be to work with the various weapons, maneuver your soldier, and utilize the various tools (loot) available to you. Plus, you'll speed up your ability to quickly build walls, ramps, stairs, and fortresses, that'll help keep you alive.

Each Season introduces new mysteries and storylines that don't always get resolved right away. For example, during Season 4, this mysterious hatch in the ground appeared within Wailing Woods. The hatch could not be opened, smashed, or altered in any way. Its purpose will likely be revealed during Season 5 or beyond.

SECTION 2

CUSTOMIZING YOUR CONTROLLER SETTINGS & CHARACTER

Starting from the Lobby screen before each match, Fortnite: Battle Royale allows you to customize your controller (or keyboard/mouse) options. Whether or not you tweak these options is a matter of personal preferences. It's not a requirement. Meanwhile, from the Locker screen, you're able to customize the appearance of your solder, assuming you've unlocked or purchased outfits and related content.

Adjusting Your Wireless Controller (Keyboard/Mouse) Settings

The default controller (or keyboard/mouse) settings offered by the game work well for most players as they first start playing Fortnite: Battle Royale. However, based on personal preferences that you'll develop while playing the game, you may opt to tweak the controller settings. To do this, from the Lobby screen, access the games Option's menu and the select the gear-shaped Settings menu.

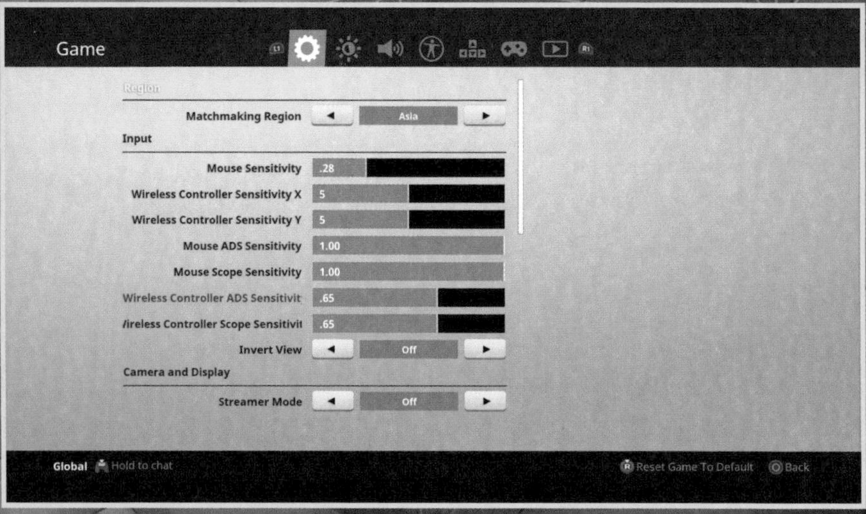

The main Settings menu is comprised of six sub-menus labeled Game, Brightness Calibration, Audio, Color Correction, Input (for Keyboard/Mouse controls), Wireless Controller, and Account.

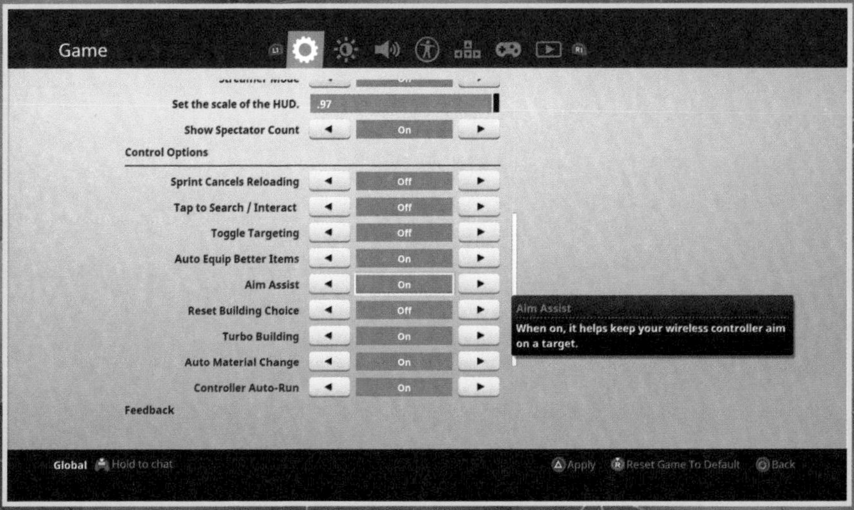

In the Game menu, it's possible to adjust options like Wireless Controller or Mouse Sensitivity. By scrolling down on this menu, you can turn on/off options like Toggle Targeting, Aim Assist, Turbo Building, Auto Material Change, and Controller Auto-Run, each of which directly impacts some aspect of the control you'll have over your character during a match.

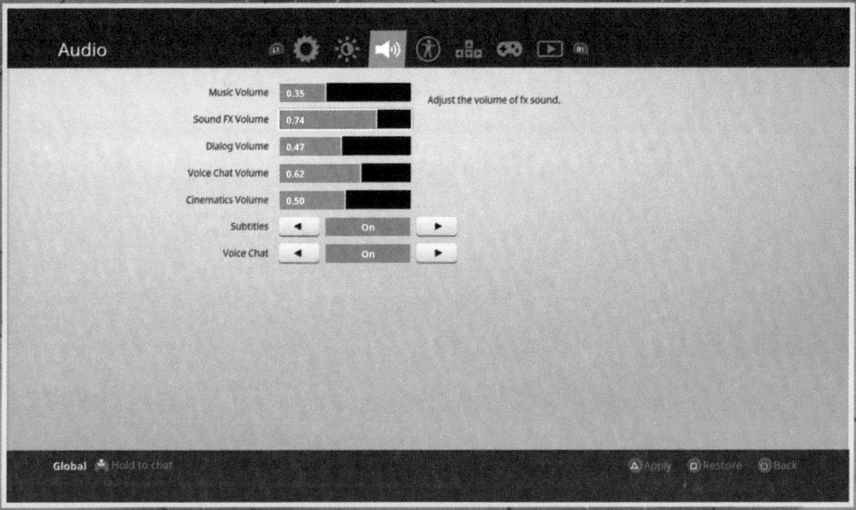

It's important to see and hear everything within the game. Based on the room lighting where you're playing and the brightness of your screen, consider manually adjusting the Brightness Calibration and sound-related options (shown on the previous page). For example, you may opt to turn up the Sound FX Volume option but turn down the Music Volume and Voice Chat Volume, since clearly hearing sounds effects in the game, like footsteps and weapons fire, is crucial.

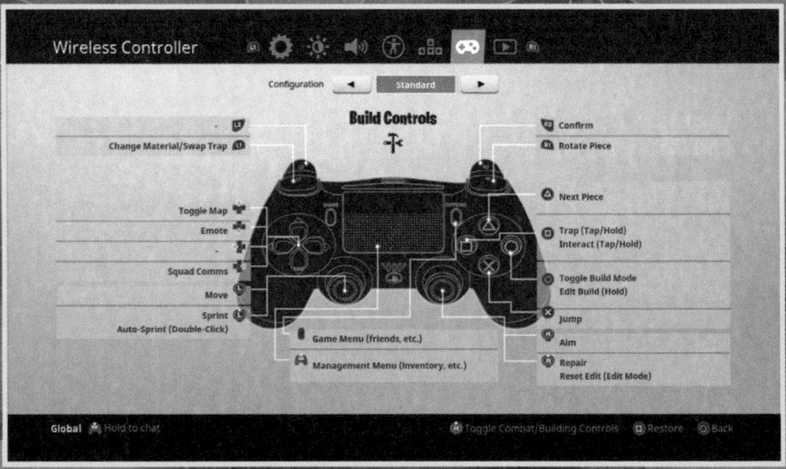

Based on the overall strategies and approach to the game you choose to adopt, by adjusting the Wireless Controller (or Keyboard/Mouse) options, it's possible to make the commands and functions you use the most, the easiest to access. For example, the Standard (or "Old School") wireless controller layout (shown on a PS4) focuses on the most commonly used gaming features.

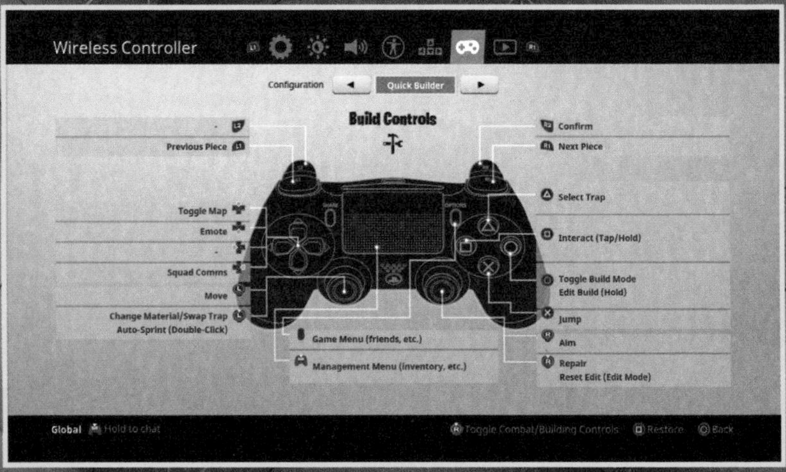

The Quick Builder (shown at the bottom of the previous page on a PS4) controller layout puts more emphasis on basic building.

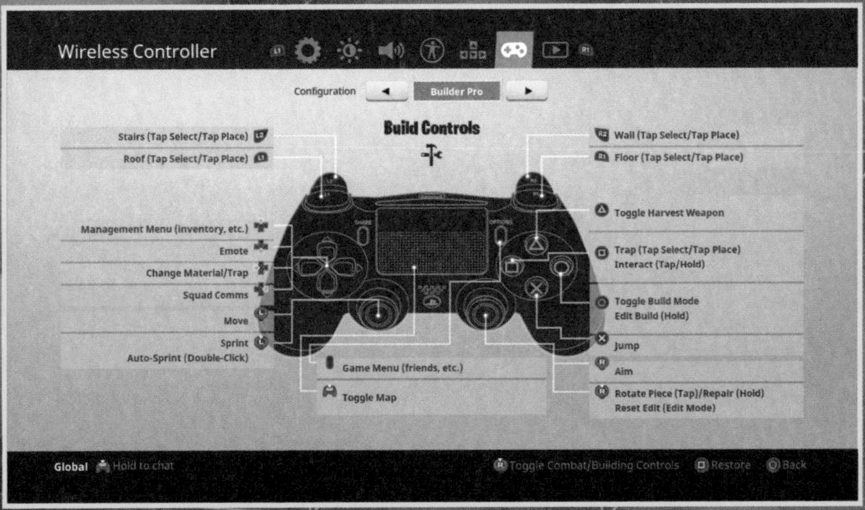

The Builder Pro controller layout (shown on the PS4) emphasizes controls used primarily for advanced building, while the Combat Pro layout makes fighting-related functions easiest to access.

If you watch a YouTube video or Twitch.tv live stream in which an expert Fortnite player talks about their controller (or keyboard/mouse) settings, the settings they talk about work for them personally, based on their motor skills, muscle memory, and their personal tastes they've developed while playing Fortnite: Battle Royale for countless hours.

Only adjust options that allow gameplay elements to work better for you personally, which you'll discover mainly through experimentation and experience. Don't just copy someone else's Settings adjustments, unless you have a good reason to do so.

Customize the Appearance of Your Soldier

There are several customizations you can make to the appearance of your soldier. Start by choosing his or her outfit. This is the clothing worn during a match. You're also able to select separate back bling, which determines the appearance of their backpack.

Next, choose the design of their glider (and related free-fall/Contrail animation), the appearance of their pickaxe, and what emotes (including dance moves) they can publically showcase during a match.

Remember, the customizations you make to your solider only impact how he/she looks in the game. You can spend real money to make your soldier appear truly awesome and unique, but this is optional.

Most gamers really appreciate the ability to customize the appearance of their soldiers. For example, you can select their outfits, back bling, glider design, pickaxe design, free fall trail animation, loading screen graphic, banner, emotes, and spray paint tag designs. Customizing your soldier's appearance can be done before each match. From the Lobby screen, access the Locker screen, and then choose the Outfit option (shown here). Only outfits you've unlocked, previously acquired, or purchased will be displayed.

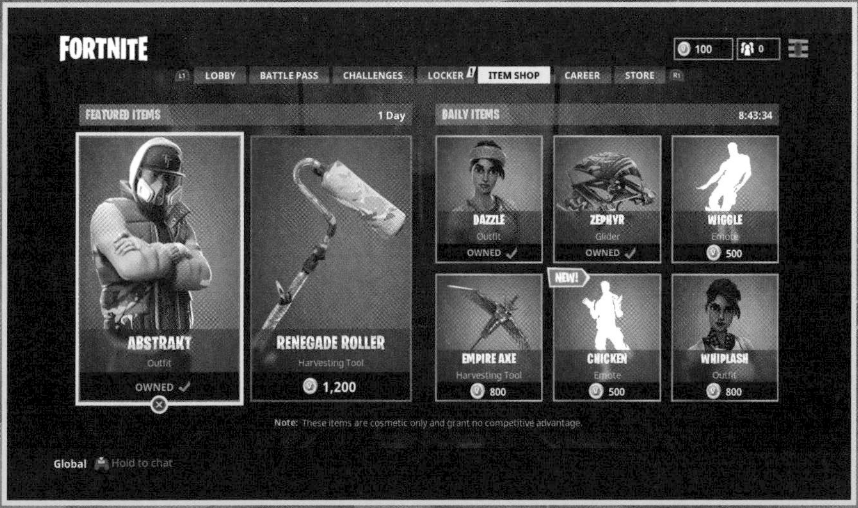

The options available to you are what you unlock during gameplay, what you purchase from the Item Shop, and what you download (for free) from Epic Game's promotional partners. Items from the Item Shop are purchased one at a time using V-Bucks.

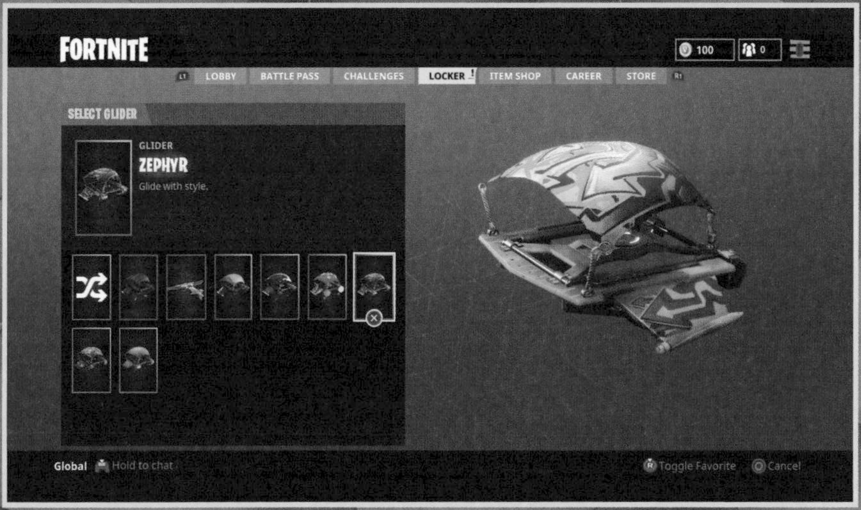

If you select the Glider option from the Locker screen, a selection of the Glider designs you've unlocked, purchased, or acquired are displayed. Choose one from the menu and confirm your choice.

Every day, a new selection of customizable options (including outfits, glider designers, pickaxe designs, and emotes), are available for sale from the Item Shop. Purchase one item at a time by exchanging V-Bucks. These items cost real money and are typically only available for a very limited time.

Plan on spending between $5.00 and $25.00 for a single outfit, or more if you want to add matching back bling and a pickaxe, for example. This optional Whiplash outfit, for example, costs 800 V-Bucks. Click on the Store menu option to purchase V-Bucks that you can exchange for items or Battle Passes. Purchasing 1,000 V-Bucks costs $9.99. Thus, this particular outfit costs approximately $8.00 (U.S.). It would be cheaper, however, to use V-Bucks you've won within the game, or to purchase 2,800 ($24.99), 7,500 ($59.99), or 13,500 ($99.99) V-Bucks at once.

SECTION 3

FORTNITE GEOGRAPHY: GET TO KNOW THE ISLAND

It's important that you discover how and when to access the island map, and that you learn how to identify key locations on the map. The island is composed of 20+ points of interest, including several new and popular destinations, which are not labeled on the map.

While you're in the pre-deployment area waiting to board the Battle Bus, or while the Battle Bus is in the air, access the island map. A blue line (composed of arrows) displays the random route the Battle Bus will take over the island, so you can more easily decide when to leave the bus and choose a preferred landing site.

While viewing the island map that shows the route that the Battle Bus will follow, start thinking about your desired landing location. Do you want to land in a less popular and more secluded area, so you can gather weapons and resources, or would you prefer to drop down into a popular part of the island, where you're sure to encounter enemy soldiers and be forced to fight almost immediately?

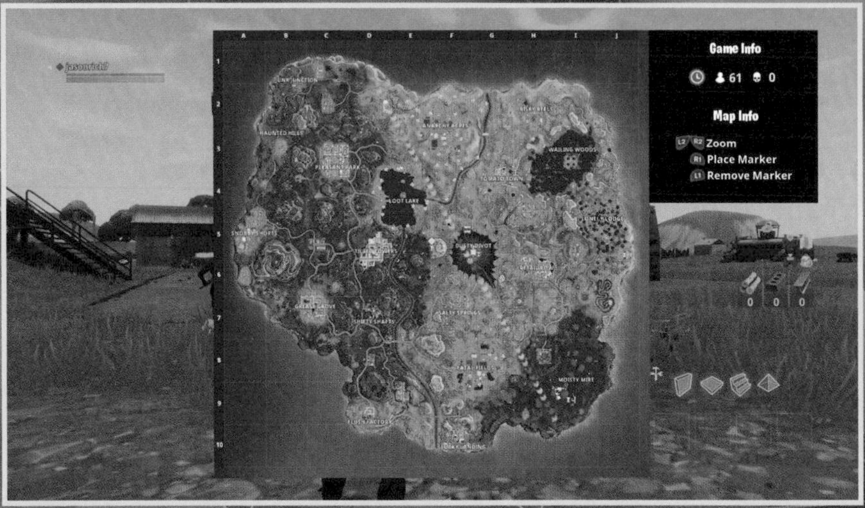

Suppose your desired landing spot is Shabby Shores (located near map coordinates A5), but when you look at the island map that shows the route the Battle Bus will take, its route takes you nowhere near this area. Now what? As with all points of interest, even if the route the Battle Bus takes does not travel directly over your desired landing location, you can move during free fall more than halfway across the entire island before your soldier's glider automatically deploys. As a result, you can almost always reach any area on the map.

At any time during a match, access the full-screen island map to figure out where you are, where you want to go, and the location of the storm. As you can see on the previous page, the portion of the island that's engulfed in the storm (and uninhabitable) is displayed in pink. The safe area is within the circle.

How to Read the Island Map

The full island map is divided into quadrants (boxes). Displayed along the top margin of the map (from left to right) are the letters "A" through "J". Along the left margin of the map, from top to bottom, are the numbers "1" through "10." Using these letters and numbers, you can easily identify any location or quadrant on the map.

For example, quadrant F2 on the map corresponds with Anarchy Acres, while coordinates H6 correspond with Retail Row. Lucky Landing can be found in quadrant G10.

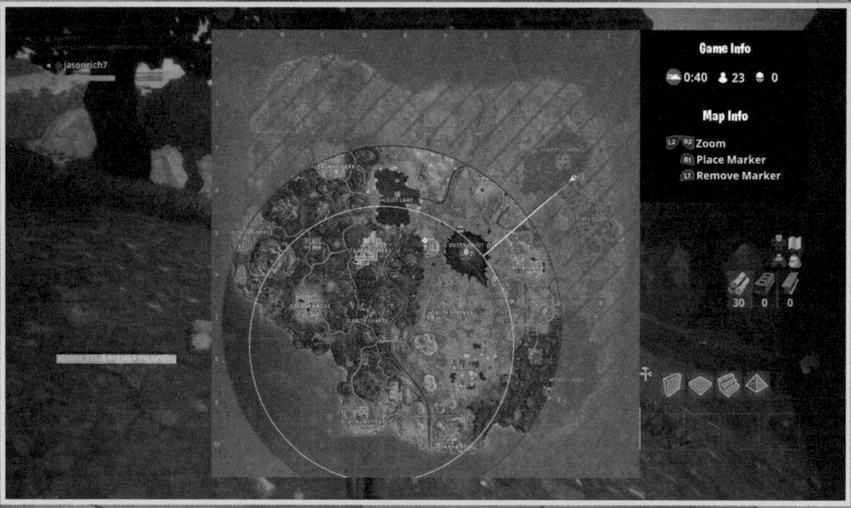

When you see two circles on the map, the outer (larger) circle represents the safe area of the island right now. The inner white circle shows where the safe area will be once the storm moves and expands again.

On the main game screen during a match, a small map is always displayed. It shows your current location. If you're outside the safe area, follow the white line that's displayed on this smaller map to reach safety as quickly as possible. Run! If you have a Launch Pad or Jetpack available, use it to make your escape and cover a lot of territory fast.

Choose the Best Moment to Jump from the Battle Bus

At the start of each match, choose when to jump off the Battle Bus as it sails across the sky, directly over the island (as seen on the previous page.)

Once you leave the Battle Bus, your solder free falls toward the island, but you can control the speed and direction they're falling. If you don't touch the controller, your soldier falls at a steady pace. Remember, the soldiers that make it safely to the ground first are at an advantage, because they can quickly grab a weapon and then start shooting unarmed adversaries as they land.

If you point your soldier downward during free fall, their falling speed increases dramatically, allowing them to reach land faster (as seen on the previous page.). If you wait too long to deploy the glider, however, it activates automatically to ensure a safe landing.

Once a glider is active, it slows a soldier's falling speed. Plus, you have more precise control over your soldier's movement during the final portion of their decent.

If you're landing in or near any point of interest (or known structure), land directly on the roof of a house, building, or structure (as seen in the previous page.) Sometimes, you'll find weapons, ammo, or loot to collect out in the open, lying on the roof. Upon landing, smash through the roof to the attic of a house, or the top floor of a building or tower. You'll often find a chest in these high-up areas, so you can quickly arm yourself before encountering enemy soldiers.

Need Directions? Check the Map

The small map that's continuously displayed on the screen and the full-size map both offer a lot of useful information when it comes to navigation and determining the safest places to go to avoid the deadly storm.

When a white line appears within the small map, this is the path to follow to avoid the moving storm. If you see a portion of the white circle displayed within this small map, this indicates that you're close to the border of uninhabitable area due to the storm. If you find yourself outside this circle once the storm moves, it's not a good situation.

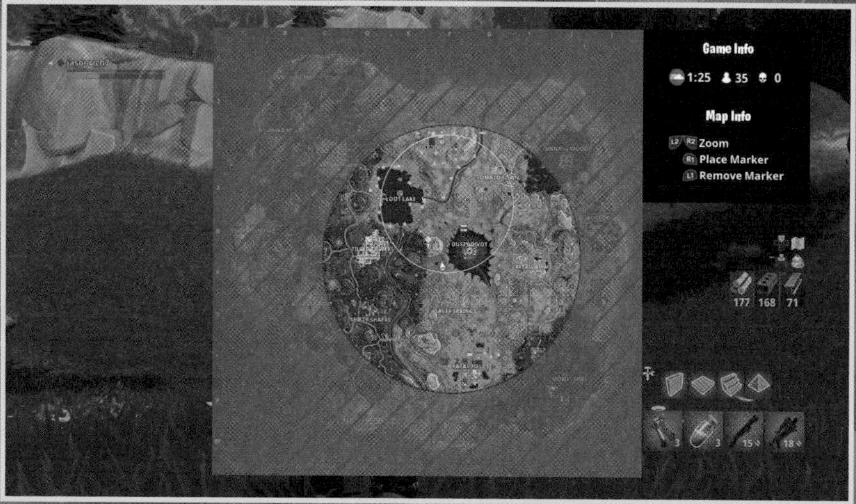

Using the full-size map, figure out where you want to go next, as well as the best route to follow, based on the direction the storm is moving, and which area of the island you want to reach. Remember, the inner white circle on the map indicates where the safe area will be after the storm moves again.

If you're defeated, don't despair. Stick around for a bit and take advantage of Spectator Mode. This allows you to kick back and watch other players compete in the match you were just eliminated from. Simply by watching other gamers explore, you'll learn a lot about various regions of the map and discover new strategies to use when engaged in fights.

Choose Your Landing Destination Like A Pro

If you watch live streams (on YouTube or Twitch.tv) of the top-ranked Fortnite players in the world, one strategy you'll often see them implement is choosing a very remote place to land once their soldier jumps from the Battle Bus. They'll further choose a landing location they know offers multiple chests that can be found and opened within moments of landing.

Anytime you choose a landing spot that's as far away as possible from the flyover route taken by the Battle Bus, and that is not near the very beginning or end of its route, you'll typically be able to land in an area that's not heavily populated with enemies. In some cases, you'll wind up alone in the area. This gives you more time to gather weapons and resources.

One ideal landing location for this strategy is between map coordinates I2.5 and J2.5 (outside of Wailing Woods and shown in the previous page.) Land on top of this house that contains a tall wooden tower on top of it. Smash your way downward using the pickaxe.

You'll discover at least two chests here.

There are also weapons, ammo, and loot to grab directly from the ground. Be sure to explore the house itself.

Chances are, you won't be able to spend too much time in this area due to the storm, but collect what you can to establish your arsenal, plus collect nearby resources.

Instead of spending time visiting the island's various points of interest, determine where the storm is headed by looking at the map, and avoid enemy soldiers early on in the match by staying exclusively in the outskirts of those popular island locations.

Along the way, visit small structures that are outside of the points of interest to collect additional weapons, ammo, and loot.

Even if you avoid points of interest, you'll likely encounter a few enemy soldiers. You can choose to fight or avoid them. As the storm continues to expand, focus on staying within the safe circle, while building your arsenal and resource collection. Do this before the circle gets really small, and you're forced to fight the remaining enemy soldiers during the End Game.

Using this strategy helps to insure you collect the weapons and resources you will need for the final battles in a match, plus it keeps you out of potentially dangerous and crowded points of interest on the map.

Among the other potential landing sites that allow you to pursue this strategy include a home found at map coordinates A6, or the llama-shaped wooden tower outside of Junk Junction (near map coordinates B1).

Discover the Island's Hotspots

In addition to the island's 20+ points of interest (as of Season 4), there are many other areas to explore that are interesting, chock-full of things to collect, and that offer their own unique challenges. The following is a summary of the island's important points of interest, as well as some of the awesome places to visit that are not labeled on the map.

Anarchy Acres

Map Coordinates: F3

This is one of two farm areas on the island. It contains barns, silos, tractors, a farmhouse, and a bunch of crop fields.

Check out the largest farmhouse and barn first, since this is where you'll discover the best weapons, ammo, loot, and chests.

Build a ramp or stairs to the second level of the stables to find a chest (shown in the previous page). Be sure to explore each of the horse stalls on the ground level, since you'll typically find worthwhile weapons and loot within several them. You can also hide from enemy soldiers within these stalls, or set Traps (or Remote Explosives) within them to more easily defeat adversaries.

Dusty Divot

Map Coordinates: G5

This is the area once known as Dusty Dunes. At the start of Season 4, it was demolished by a comet. The problem with this area is that it's centrally located on the map and very popular. As a result, you'll definitely encounter many enemy soldiers here, so be ready to fight.

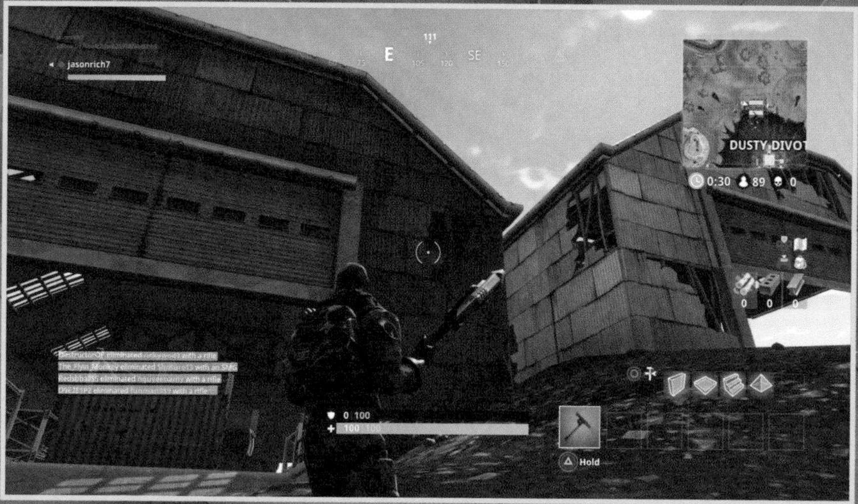

There are two large buildings (warehouses) on the outskirts of the crater. While you'll be able to stock up on weapons, ammo, and loot, plus find a few chests, you'll often have to fight enemy soldiers in order to stay alive.

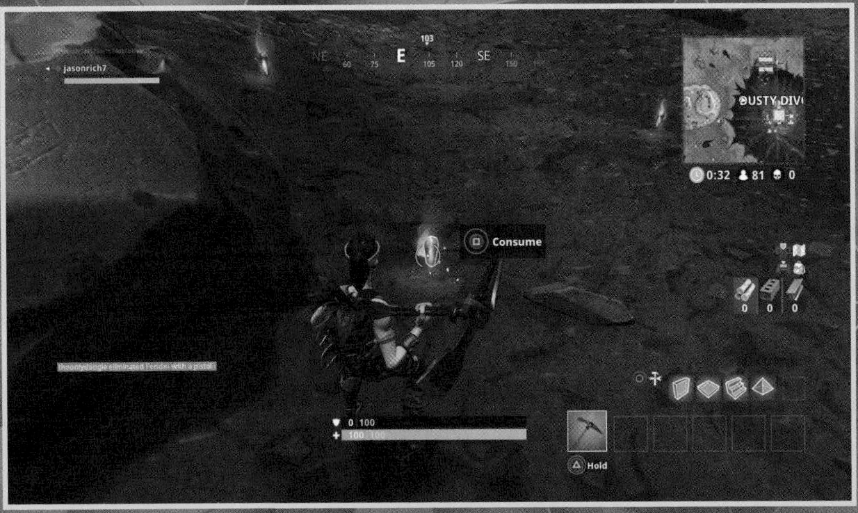

Within the crater itself are Hop Rocks. When a soldier consumes one of these, for about 30 seconds, he'll be able to jump higher and leap farther. This ability can be used to your tactical advantage, to quickly approach enemies and launch an ambush. However, if your enemies consume Hop Rocks, it'll give them superpowers as well, which can be used against you.

In the center of the massive crater is a secret research facility. Once you enter, you'll need to navigate through maze-like tunnels to reach the various offices and labs.

Behind each closed door, you may find a lab that's filled with useful items to collect, or you could discover an enemy soldier waiting to pummel you with their weapons, so be prepared for whatever you encounter, and keep your weapon drawn.

Located in the center of the research lab is the comet, which is apparently being studied, or perhaps its power is somehow being harnessed. The secrets this comet holds will likely be revealed during Season 5. In the meantime, what will happen to Dusty Divot in the future is anyone's guess.

Fatal Fields

Map Coordinates: G8.5

As you explore this region, you'll discover that it's a second, rather large farming area. The farmhouse, silos, barn, and stable, as well as the farm's other structures, are far apart. To reach each of them, you'll need to spend time out in the open and will be vulnerable to attack. Be prepared to hide behind objects, or build walls to use as shields, in case you're attacked.

Anytime you're out in the open and need to travel a great distance, run fast, in a zigzag and unpredictable formation, and keep jumping in order to make yourself a difficult target to hit.

Inside the large barn (shown on the previous page), you'll discover piles of hay. You can hide behind hay, but it offers no protective shielding. By smashing or shooting at the hay, you'll sometimes discover useful goodies. However, there could just as easily be an enemy soldier waiting to launch an attack from behind a haystack.

Search the large farmhouse carefully. Inside the bathroom, smash your way into a hidden room that contains a chest.

Flush Factory

Map Coordinates: D9.5

This is an abandoned, multi-level toilet factory. Inside, explore the manufacturing area, as well as the offices and restrooms. There's plenty of useful loot to find and gather inside.

Inside the factory, build stairs or a ramp to reach the top of these restrooms, where you'll discover a chest.

Located near Flush Factory, near map coordinates E9, are a group of buildings that aren't labeled on the map.

The building with the red ropes outside is a dance club. You can spend time dancing on the dance floor, but you'll be more productive if you search the area for loot.

There's a chest located behind the DJ booth.

Each of the other buildings in this area also offer useful weapons, ammo, loot, and occasionally chests. Be sure to check the trucks and metal containers found on the streets in this area.

Greasy Grove

Map Coordinates: C7

Fast food restaurants, a few stores, and homes are what you'll encounter in this region of the island.

Explore the buildings to find loot and potentially hide from enemies. You can also place Traps or Remote Explosives within the buildings to surprise enemies with a painful blast. If you don't yet have a Trap, one might be for sale from the Vending Machine (shown on the previous page.)

It's in the attics and basements (if any) of the homes that you'll find chests and other useful weapons, ammo, and loot. Land on a roof and smash your way down, enter a home through a door and work your way up; or from the outside, build a ramp to the top of the roof and smash your way down. Don't forget to search the stores as well (shown above).

Anytime you come across a front door to a home (or building) that's already open (as seen on the previous page), it means someone else has been inside...and they could still be there. Listen carefully for footsteps or the sounds of enemies smashing through walls, for example.

If someone has already opened the chests and collected the weapons inside, a search of the home or building will not be too productive. Instead, consider waiting for the enemy soldier to leave, and then launch an attack. If you win, you'll be able to collect their weapons, ammo, loot, and resources, including what they just gathered from the house or building.

Sometimes, chests can be found outside, out in the open, or hidden within a small structure, like this doghouse.

If you get ambushed and happen to have collected a Port-A-Fort, activate it to instantly build a multi-level metal fort that offers protection. When you climb to the top, you'll typically have a perfect vantage point from which to shoot enemies below.

Located a short distance from Greasy Grove is a sports complex that's not labeled on the map. You'll find it near coordinates C5.

There's an indoor swimming pool here. Explore it, and you'll likely find at least one chest, as well as plenty of other weapons, ammo, and loot.

The indoor soccer field and the rooms and areas which surround it are also chock full of useful loot to collect.

Haunted Hills

Map Coordinates: B3

The churches, crypts, and graveyard in this relatively small region provide an ideal setting for shootouts. There's also great scavenging to be done here for chests, weapons, ammo, loot, and stone.

Be sure to explore the basements and tower within the churches.

Inside the churches (shown on the previous page), smash through the stone walls to reveal hidden crypts and rooms that typically contain a chest or loot.

Each church typically contains at least one or two chests.

From the higher levels of a church, choose a sniping location, crouch down (to achieve better aim), and then use a shotgun, long-range rifle, or sniper rifle (with a scope) to target enemy soldiers below.

Junk Junction

Map Coordinates: Between B1.5 and C1.5

Junk cars and garbage are piled up everywhere within Junk Junction. You'll often find items to collect on top of car and garbage piles. On the ground, between the piles, is a maze-like area to explore.

Outside of Junk Junction (near map coordinates B1), be sure to explore this llama-shaped tower to find several chests and other weapons. If possible, after leaving the Battle Bus, land on top of this tower and smash your way down.

It’s safer to explore Junk Junction (shown on the previous page) from higher levels as opposed to ground level, especially if there are enemies lurking around the area. Either climb to the top of junk piles and jump between them, or build bridges that’ll help you stay on the high ground.

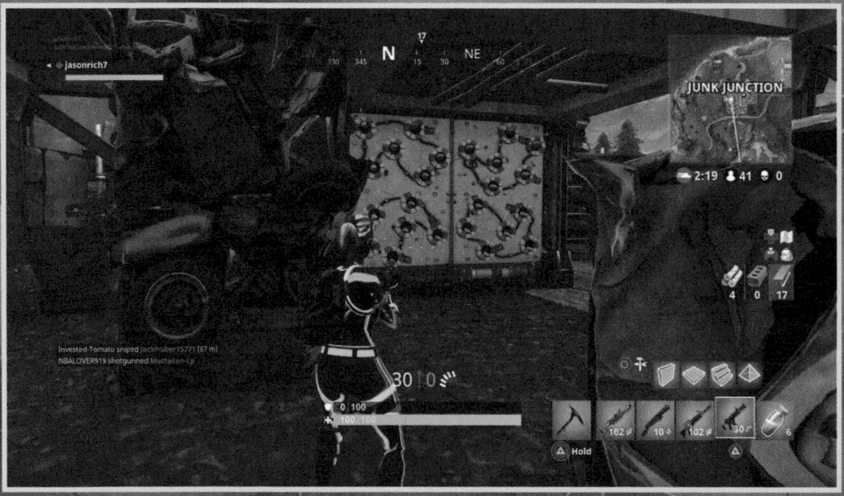

Consider placing a Trap or Remote Explosive on ground level near the car piles. As an enemy soldier explores the maze-like area, you can defeat them with a surprise explosion, while you’re a safe distance away.

Be sure to explore the buildings in the Junk Junction area, as well as the structures you’ll discover just outside of Junk Junction, near map coordinates C1.

Lonely Lodge

Map Coordinates: J5

You may think of camping as a relaxing activity. However, it's anything but relaxing here in Lonely Lodge, where you'll find a lodge, a collection of cabins, parked RVs, and a tall observation tower.

The most exciting place to explore within this point of interest is this massive waterfront mansion (found at map coordinates J5).

As you approach the front door of the mansion (shown in the previous page), use the pickaxe to smash the ground. You'll discover the entrance to a hidden basement that contains some type of high-tech control center that's filled with awesome items to collect. There are several chests to be found here.

Within Lonely Lodge, be sure to explore the main lodge. You'll find chests and other goodies inside.

The tallest structure in the area is this wooden observation tower. It can be seen on the previous page near the top, in particular, you'll find some great loot. If you climb to the top, don't fall or jump off, or you'll perish. However, if you engage an enemy soldier in a fight near the top of this tower, try to force them to jump or fall over the edge.

Many of the small cabins in the area contain weapons, ammo, and loot. You can easily booby trap one or more of these cabins with Traps or Remote Explosives, or hide inside, close the door behind you, crouch down, draw your weapon, and wait for an enemy soldier to enter. When they do, ambush them!

Loot Lake

Map Coordinates: E4

In the middle of the lake, there's an island that contains a house. Inside, you'll discover chests and other useful items to collect. Then, make your way to the rowboat in the center of the lake, as well as the buildings (located near docks) on the opposite side of the lake.

Instead of walking through the lake to cross it (which is a slow process that leaves you out in the open and exposed to potential enemy attacks), build a bridge over the water. Once you start crossing the water on foot, however, you can't start building a bridge in the middle of the water. The bridge needs to begin on land.

If you attempt to reach the rowboat in the lake, empty the chest quickly and be prepared to evade enemy fire. If you have a sniper rifle (or rifle with a scope), stay on land and shoot at enemy soldiers who attempt to reach the rowboat.

The house on the island is chock-full of items worth collecting, so search carefully, but be prepared to encounter enemy soldiers.

The two buildings located near the docks are both worth searching, although you're more apt to find chests and useful loot in the larger of the buildings. As you approach either building, watch out for snipers.

After climbing the stairs of the larger building, you'll discover a chest in this loft area. You'll need to build a ramp (or stairs) to reach it.

Lucky Landing

Map Coordinates: Between F10 and G10

The buildings in and around this point of interest all have an Asian influence. Within the building that contains the giant pink tree, you're apt to find rare and powerful weapons. However, be sure to explore all of the buildings, bridges, and towers in this region.

The bridge on the previous page leads to Lucky Landing offers weapons, ammo, and loot to collect, both within the bridge and below it.

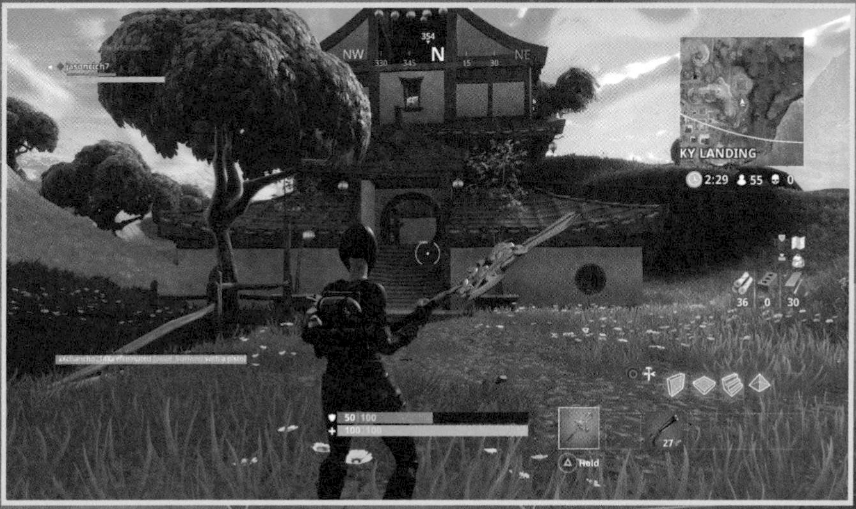

There's a chest to be found in the main room of this Asian temple.

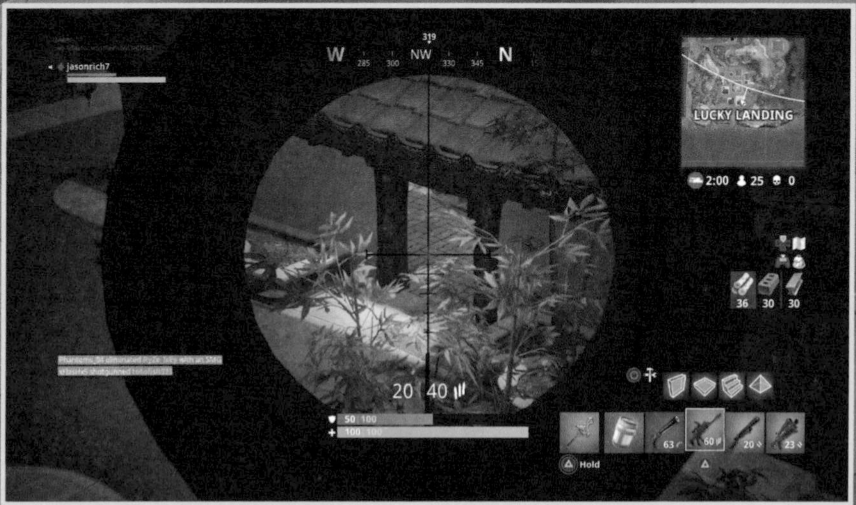

Go to the top floor of this office building. In addition to finding items within the building, the large window on the top floor offers a great view of the area, from which you can use a rifle to shoot at enemy soldiers below. Targeting enemies on the ground is easier with a rifle that has a scope, but any rifle or shotgun should do the trick. As always, a head shot causes much more damage than a body shot.

Look behind the counters, and everywhere else in stores and restaurants to find chests. Check the shelves for ammo boxes. On the floor of almost every building in this area, you'll discover weapons, ammo, or loot waiting to be grabbed.

Moisty Mire

Map Coordinates: I9

This region contains lots of trees that make up a dense forest. Located near the outskirts of Moisty Mire is an abandoned prison.

Within the prison area, search the guard towers, and then make your way to the individual prison cells.

Smash through walls in the prison cells and you'll discover offices, guard rooms, and other areas you can't otherwise reach.

Just outside the prison, you'll encounter a bunch of vehicles. Two of them contain chests.

Also located in this area is a movie set. Explore this area, where you'll find several buildings, a wooden observation tower, a swamp that contains a rowboat, and other interesting places to visit.

The wooden observation tower contains a chest. This is also a good location from which you can shoot at enemies from above.

Be sure to locate the chest hidden within the tree near the movie set. There may also be an additional chest in the rowboat that's floating in the swamp. While reaching it, however, you'll be out in the open and vulnerable to attack, so proceed with caution.

Pleasant Park

Map Coordinates: C3

In addition to Snobby Shores, this is an area of the island that contains a bunch of single-family homes. There's also a park and sports field here.

This is a popular area, so if you're not the first person to reach the center of the soccer field to open the chest, avoid this open area, or you'll get shot.

The structure in the center of town often contains a chest, as well as a central location from which you can shoot at enemies in all directions around you.

Build a mini-fort above the structure in the center of town, and you'll have a 360-degree view of the area. Using a shotgun, a sniper rifle, or any rifle with a scope, you'll be able to pick off enemy soldiers with relative ease without having to move around too much.

As with any home on the island, the best approach is to land on the roof, or build a ramp from the outside to the roof, and smash your way down through the attic using your pickaxe. Inside the homes, you'll likely encounter enemy soldiers, so listen carefully for their footsteps and movements.

Retail Row

Map Coordinates: H5.5

This area contains a handful of shops, restaurants, a water tower and a few homes, most of which surround street parking areas. One of the unique things about this region is that chests are not always found in the same place.

You'll often discover a chest at the top of the water tower.

From the roof of this home, located near the end of Retail Row, smash you way downward. This home is missing a piece of its roof. If you look carefully, you'll spot a chest from above. If you know an enemy is hiding in a house or structure and you have explosive weapons at your disposal (such as a grenade launcher or Remote Explosive), blow up or destroy that house or structure. The enemy will likely perish.

Smash the cars and trucks in this area to collect metal, or crouch behind them and use them for shielding if you're getting shot at while exploring this area.

Most of the stores and restaurants have weapons, ammo, and loot lying out in the open, on the ground, waiting to be collected. However, look for hidden rooms and areas where additional items, including chests, may also be available.

In the market, walk through the loading door, and then climb up on boxes and shelves. Near the ceilings, you'll find a chest.

Risky Reels

Map Coordinates: H2

This is one of the new points of interest added to the map in conjunction with Season 4. Here, you'll find a drive-in movie theater. In the parking lot are a bunch of abandoned cars and trucks.

Check the backs of trucks for chests and loot, and then explore the area near the movie screen, as well as the nearby buildings.

Go inside the concession stand (snack shop). A chest can be found inside the bathroom stalls, so watch for its golden glow.

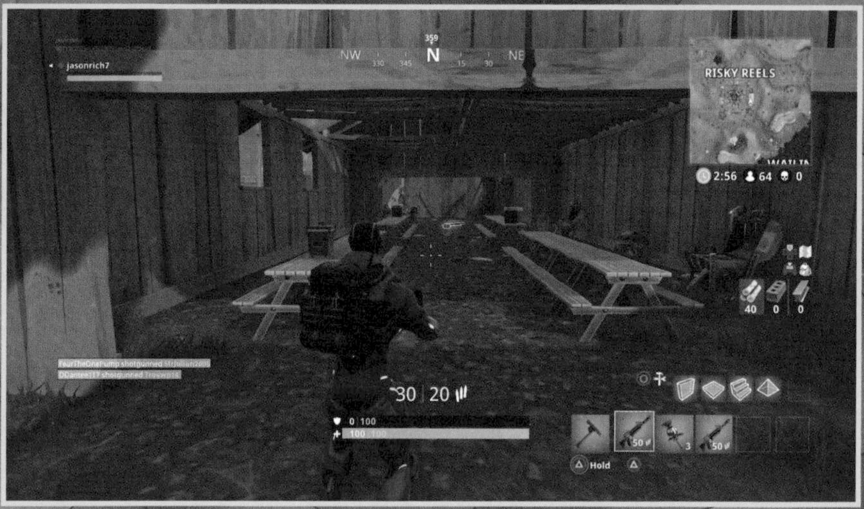

In the large shed containing picnic tables, you'll often find a chest, as well as other weapons and loot lying out in the open.

There's an old house located near the drive-in theater. Explore it like you would any house, and you'll likely find plenty of weapons, ammo, and loot, not to mention a chest in the attic.

Salty Springs

Map Coordinates: F7

A group of single-family homes and a gas station are clustered together in this area. Be sure to search the homes, but be on the lookout for enemy soldiers who may be lurking within them.

The homes in Salty Springs and throughout the island may all look different from the outside, but inside, most have several floors, each with a handful of rooms. While you'll likely find weapons, ammo, and loot out in the open (on the ground) within the various rooms, it's often in the attics and basements that you'll find chests.

The stone structure above is definitely worth visiting, especially if you need to find and grab some weapons. The stone structure is also heavily fortified, so it makes a good hiding place if you need one.

Always be on the lookout for Supply Drops (shown on the previous page.). They typically land just outside of points of interest on the map. When you discover one landing nearby, approach with caution, and only if you need to expand your arsenal with some potentially powerful and rare weapons.

Instead of approaching a Supply Drop, many experienced players find a good hiding spot near the landing site and wait to ambush enemy soldiers who attempt to reach the Supply Drop. Any long-range weapon, particularly a sniper rifle (or rifle with a scope), or a grenade launcher, can be used to launch a surprise attack from a distance. If you have access to a Launch Pad, use it to quickly reach an adversary from a distance, and then launch a close-range attack when you land.

Shifty Shafts

Map Coordinates: D7

In addition to the buildings and structures you can see above ground, this region contains a maze-like collection of underground mining tunnels.

There are structures and areas to explore outside of Shifty Shafts that can provide a decent collection of weapons, ammo, and loot. For example, there's this Battle Bus which crash-landed here.

There are a few homes on the outskirts of Shifty Shafts to explore. Each contains items worth collecting.

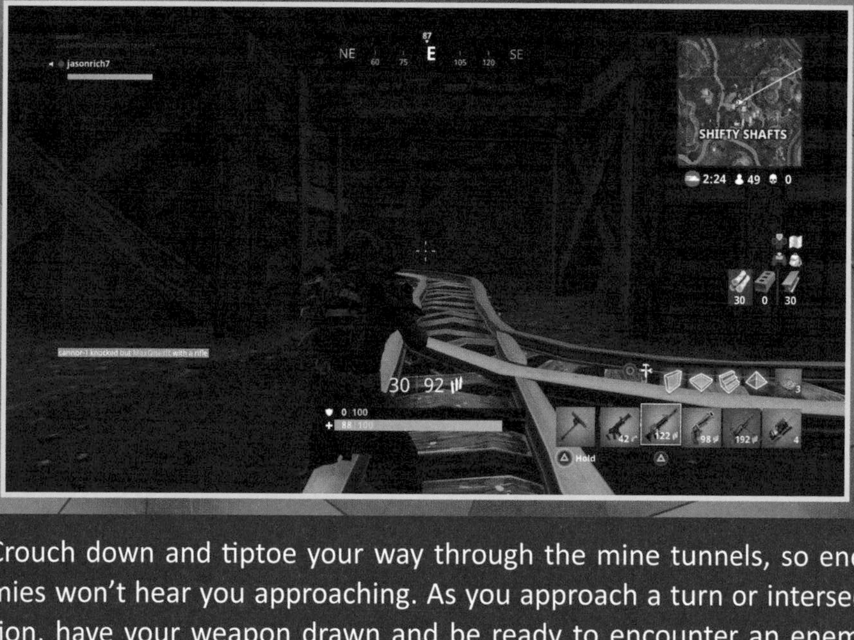

Crouch down and tiptoe your way through the mine tunnels, so enemies won't hear you approaching. As you approach a turn or intersection, have your weapon drawn and be ready to encounter an enemy soldier who's also exploring this region.

You'll find chests, as well as weapons, ammo, and loot on the ground within the mine tunnels. If you see a crate to stand on, do so. Always remember that you have the advantage by being even slightly higher than your opponent when you engage in a firefight.

Stock up on resources, and then go on a mini shopping spree when you encounter this Vending Machine. What's offered will be a random selection of rare and powerful weapons and/or loot.

Snobby Shores

Map Coordinates: A5

This is where the rich people who formally populated the island once lived. The area contains several lovely waterfront mansions, each of which offers multiple floors and many rooms to explore. Located near this region are two mountains. In Season 4, one mountain has a secret base hidden inside it, while the other contains a home. (This base may be removed from the game in Season 5 or later.)

Follow the roads to travel between the mansions in this area, or smash through the stone walls and security fences to take a shortcut.

In addition to searching the mansions, be sure to search the security buildings and storage buildings location near many of the mansions (shown on the previous page.).

Don't forget to search the attics and basements (if applicable) of each mansion. This is typically where you'll discover chests.

Before entering any mansion or home, listen carefully for noises coming from the inside. Also, peek through the windows, and make sure the coast is clear. Don't forget, you can always surprise an enemy by shooting through a window. If you know someone is already inside, and you're not afraid to confront them, consider entering any mansion or home through the garage or back door, as opposed to the front door. Be unpredictable.

Within the mountain at map coordinates C5.5, you'll discover a hidden base. Build a ramp to the top of this hill, and then smash open the garage door of the hut at the top. Enter inside and drop down into the heart of the mountain.

Explore the entire area of this hidden base. You'll find several chests, along with plenty of other weapons, ammo, and loot. There's also a giant missile here (see the previous page.). The purpose of this base and the missile are a mystery that might be revealed during Season 5. In the meantime, be careful of enemies who are also wondering through this area.

Tilted Towers

Map Coordinates: D5.5

The first thing you'll notice when you enter Tilted Towers is that it's one of the most popular places on the island, so you're sure to encounter many enemy soldiers here. Be prepared to fight your way through each of the buildings. Also, be ready to protect yourself when you're on the ground walking or running on the roads.

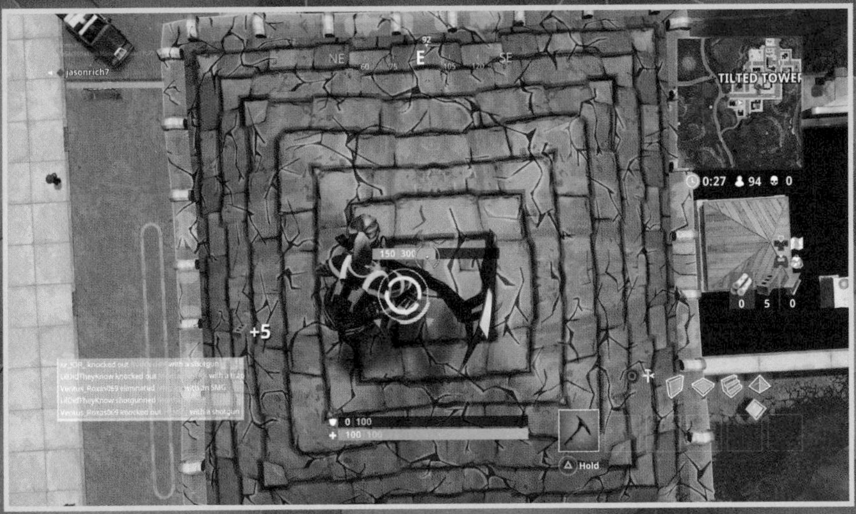

If you're planning to land in this area from the Battle Bus, be the first person to wind up on the roof of the clock tower, and then smash your way down toward ground level. Along the way, you'll discover at least three chests.

To easily defeat a few enemies here in Tilted Towers, find a safe position near the top of a building, and then use a shotgun, a sniper rifle, or a rifle with a scope to shoot at enemies below. Notice that there's an unopened chest within the window in the building across from this soldier. Simply aim your weapon at the chest and wait for an unsuspecting enemy to approach and open it. As soon as you see the enemy in your sights, start shooting.

When exploring the various buildings, look for hidden rooms, attics, and basements.

Stick to the higher ground here in Tilted Tower. If you're forced to be at ground level, especially if you're out in the open, be prepared to build a wall for shielding quickly. There are items to be found outside, on the ground, if you're brave enough to go after them.

Each building contains multiple floors and several rooms. Don't be surprised if you find enemies hiding. Be extra cautious if you enter a room after hearing footsteps or the sound of a door opening or closing.

Tomato Town

Map Coordinates: G4

Aside from a pizza restaurant, taco stand, and gas station, this area contains several homes to explore. The interesting parts of this point of interest are the tunnels and bridges that lead into and out of this region.

Check out both levels of the pizza restaurant. An assortment of random weapons, ammo, and loot can be found here.

Inside various homes (shown here and on the previous page), you're apt to find chests and other goodies.

Anytime you see a home with a cellar door on the outside, smash open the door and explore each room of the basement. You will almost always find a chest.

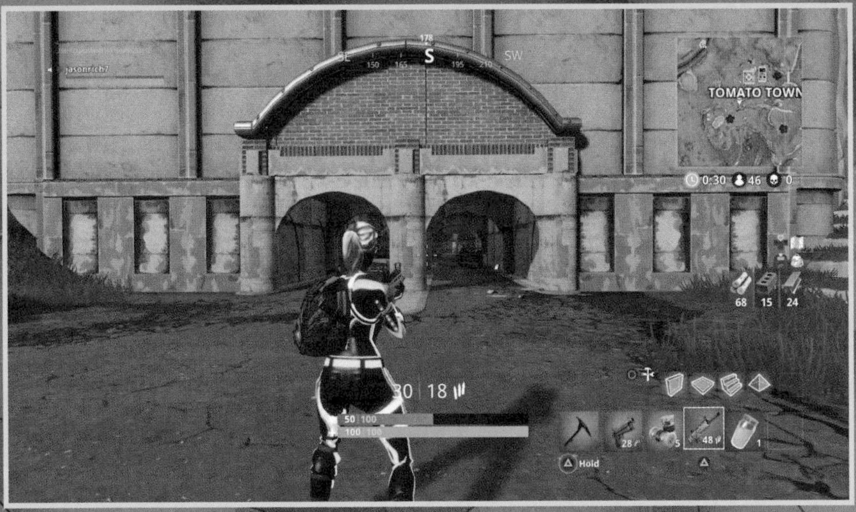

After entering into this tunnel, proceed through the door (about half way through the tunnel) and climb the stairs.

Wailing Woods

Map Coordinates: I3

Here, be sure to collect plenty of wood using your pickaxe. In the center of this area is a hedge maze. Make your way through the maze to discover wooden structures that contain items worth collecting.

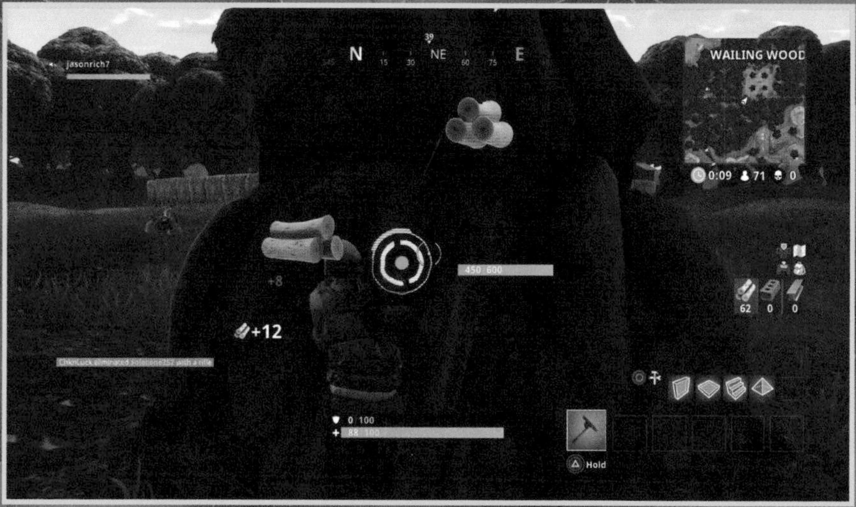

Smash the trees to collect wood, or if there are any soldiers in the area, hide behind larger trees and use them as shielding. The trees with thick trunks generate a lot of wood.

Near the center of Wailing Woods, you'll stumble upon the entrance to the hedge maze. This is shown on the previous page.

Follow the hedge maze in search of the tower. Along the way, be on the lookout for chests, weapons, and, of course, enemy soldiers who may be hiding around any turn.

Search the tower to find chests and other loot.

Climb on top of the hedges so you're higher up than soldiers walking through the maze. This makes it easier to get clear shots.

If you're reaching Wailing Woods directly from the Battle Bus, land directly on the roof of the wooden tower.

To get a great bird's-eye view from above, build a ramp and then a platform directly over the hedge maze.

Take a short detour to the outskirts of Wailing Woods, and you'll discover this massive wooden tower near the coastline. Find the secret door, go inside, climb upwards, and collect the loot that's inside!

Anytime you're traveling through areas that are outside of the island's various points of interest, be sure to investigate any small structures you discover. Inside you'll sometimes find useful weapons, ammo, and loot. This small hut, for example, has a basement that's definitely worth checking out.

SECTION 4

THERE'S AN ARSENAL OF WEAPONS AVAILABLE ON THE ISLAND

At any given time, the island contains hundreds of different types of weapons to collect, store in your backpack, and then use against adversaries.

The weapon categories these firearms and explosives typically fall into include: Assault Rifles, Crossbows, Grenade Launchers, Grenades, Miniguns, Pistols, Rocket Launchers, Shotguns, SMGs (Sub Machine Guns), and Sniper Rifles.

Many Fortnite gamers agree that the most useful weapon to master is any type of shotgun. There are many types to choose from, and shotguns are more powerful than pistols. When you view the Backpack Inventory screen, details about the selected weapon/item you're holding are displayed. Here, details about the Tactical Shotgun are displayed.

Shotguns can be used in close-range or mid-range combat situations, or even at a distance. (From a distance, they're harder to aim accurately than a rifle with a scope, for example.) When using a shotgun, always try for a headshot to inflict the most damage.

Each category of weapon can be used for a different purpose. Based on the type of enemy encounter you're experiencing at any given moment, it's essential that you choose the most appropriate weapon at your disposal.

Before engaging in a firefight, consider:

- The types of weapons currently in your backpack and available to you.
- The amount of ammo you currently have for each weapon. (Be sure to pick up as much ammo as you can throughout each match.)
- The distance between you and your opponent.
- Your surroundings, and whether or not your weapon will need to destroy a barrier, fortress wall, or shielding before it can inflict damage on an enemy.
- Your own skill level as a gamer, and your speed when it comes to selecting, targeting/aiming, and then firing your weapon.

In each weapon category, up to a dozen or more different types of weapons may become accessible to you. Epic Games regularly tweaks the selection of weapons available, as well as the capabilities of each weapon.

A powerful weapon with no ammo is useless. Collect ammo from chests, Supply Drops, Ammo Boxes (shown on the previous page), that you find lying on the ground, and that you collect from defeated enemies.

Three Tips to Improve Your Shooting Accuracy

Regardless of the weapon you're using, your aim improves when you're crouching down.

While it's often necessary to run or jump while you're firing a weapon, your accuracy improves when you're standing still.

You almost always have an advantage when you're higher up than your opponent and shooting in a downward direction.

Understand How Weapons Are Rated and Categorized

While every weapon has the ability to cause damage and defeat your adversaries, each is rated based on several criteria, including its rarity. Weapons are color-coded with a hue around them to showcase their rarity.

Weapons with a **gray** hue are "Common."

Weapon with a **green** hue are "Uncommon."

Weapons with a **blue** hue are "Rare."

Weapons with a **purple** hue are "Epic."

"Legendary" weapons (with an **orange** hue) are hard to find, extra powerful, and very rare. If you're able to obtain one, grab it!

It is possible to collect several of the same weapon, but each could have a different rarity. So, if you collect two of the same weapon, and one is rare, but the second is legendary, definitely keep the legendary weapon and trade the other for something else when you find a replacement.

The rarity of a weapon contributes heavily to its Damage Per Second (DPS) Rating. Thus, the DPS Rating for a legendary weapon is much higher than the DPS Rating for an identical weapon that has a common rarity, for example.

- **DPS Rating—**This stands for "Damage Per Second." Use this rating to help estimate a weapon's power. It does not take into account things like the accuracy of your aim or the extra damage you can inflict by making a headshot. In general, DPS is calculated by multiplying the damage the weapon can cause by its fire rate.
- **Damage Rating—**A numeric rating based on how much potential damage a weapon can cause per direct hit.
- **Fire Rate—**This refers to the number of bullets fired per second. Some of the most powerful weapons have a slow Fire Rate, so to inflict the most damage, your aim needs to be perfect. Otherwise, during the time between shots, your enemy could move or launch their own counter-attack.
- **MAG (Magazine) Capacity—**This is the total number of ammunition rounds (or bullets) the weapon can hold at once. Reloading a weapon takes valuable time, during which your soldier will be vulnerable to attack. Your enemy could also move, meaning you'll need to re-aim your weapon.
- **Reload Time—**The number of seconds it takes to reload the weapon, assuming you have replacement ammo available. Some of the most powerful weapons have a very slow reload time, so if your shooting accuracy isn't great, you'll be at a disadvantage.

There are plenty of websites, including: IGN.com (www.ign.com/wikis/fortnite/Weapons), Gameskinny.com (www.gameskinny.com/9mt22/complete-fortnite-battle-royale-weapons-stats-list), and RankedBoost.com (https://rankedboost.com/fortnite/best-weapons-tier-list), that provide the current stats for each weapon offered in Fortnite, based on the latest tweaks made to the game. Just make sure, when you look at this information online, that it refers to the most recently released version of Fortnite: Battle Royale.

Choose Your Arsenal Wisely

Based on where you are, what challenges you're currently encountering, and what you anticipate your needs will be, stock your backpack with the weapons and tools you believe you'll need. For example, as you prepare for the final fights at the end of a match, a sniper rifle and grenade/rocket launcher are essential. You'll likely be hiding in your fortress and trying to defeat the final enemies who are hiding in their own fortress. The weapons you use must be able to destroy fortress walls, plus inflict damage on your enemies.

If during those final minutes of a match an enemy rushes you (or uses a Launch Pad to get close quickly), be prepared to engage in close or mid-range combat. Having a Chug Jug (or other HP and shield power-up essentials) on hand could keep you alive if you're harmed in battle.

At any time, your soldier's backpack can hold six items (including the pickaxe). That leaves five slots in which you can carry different types of guns, alternative weapons (such as a Trap, Remote Explosive, or Grenades), and/or loot (such as Med Kits, Chug Jugs, Shield Potions, Bandages, or Slurp Juice). Make smart inventory decisions throughout each match. The Backpack Inventory screen allows you to view what you have, plus organize the backpack's contents.

SECTION 5

DISCOVER TYPES OF LOOT ON THE ISLAND

Just as powerful weapons and ammo can be found throughout the island, a selection of loot is also available. Loot can help boost your HP, increase your shields, or provide additional weapons or tools that will help you stay alive. Epic Games continuously adds new types of loot to the game.

Descriptions of Loot Items

As of May 2018, the following is a list of loot you'll likely encounter on the island. Some items are considered rare, and much harder to find than others.

Apples—You'll discover Apples under trees, scattered randomly around the island. For each Apple that's consumed, a soldier's HP increases by five.

Bandages—Each time a bandage is used, it replenishes 15 HP. A player can carry up to 5 bandages within their backpack in a single slot. It takes several seconds to use bandages, during which time a soldier is vulnerable to attack, so be sure you're well-hidden or protected when using this item.

Boogie Bombs—Toss one of these bombs at an opponent and they'll be forced to dance for 5 seconds while taking damage.

Bush—A bush can be worn by a soldier and used as camouflage. Be sure to crouch down to avoid being seen. If there are other bushes in the area, you'll blend right in. However, a bush offers no protection from attacks. If you start moving while camouflaged by a bush, an adversary will definitely notice and attack. This item is best used outside, when standing still, to avoid being detected by nearby enemies.

Cozy Campfires—Once the Cozy Campfire is activated, any soldiers who stands next to it will gain 2 HP per second for up to 25 seconds (up to 50 HP). The drawback is that a soldier is vulnerable to attack during this time, so activate the campfire after building a protective barrier around yourself and the campfire, or find a secure and secluded place to use it.

If you're playing with teammates, multiple people can take advantage of the campfire's healing powers. When you stand next to the flame, look for the "+" icons that appear so you know it's working.

Chug Jugs—This item takes 15 seconds to drink, during which time a soldier is vulnerable to attack unless he/she's protected. Consuming a Chug Jug restores a soldier's HP *and* shield meter to 100 percent. Drink one of these as you enter into later stages of a match, when survival becomes more difficult.

Clingers—When you throw one of these plunger-shaped grenades at an enemy, it sticks to them and then explodes.

Grenades—Toss a grenade at an enemy, and it'll explode on impact. Direct hits cause the most damage, but even if the grenade lands close to an enemy, damage is still inflicted.

Impulse Grenades—This type of grenade inflicts damage on enemies and throws them into the air, away from the point of impact.

Launch Pads—Activate this item to catapult your solider into the air, and then automatically deploy their glider. You can then guide them around in mid-air for a few seconds. Use this tool, for example, to escape after being engulfed by the storm, or to flee from an attack. It allows you to move great distances quickly. While you're flying, you can still be shot at by enemies.

Small Shield Potions—Consuming this item increases your shield strength by 25, but it takes several seconds to drink, during which time your soldier is vulnerable to attack.

Med Kits—Restore your health to one hundred percent each time a Med Kit (shown on the previous page) is used. It takes ten seconds to use a Med Kit, during which time your solider is vulnerable to attack.

Port-A-Fort—This insta-fort is made of metal, and is instantly built when you activate it. Use it for protection without the need for manual building. It requires no resources.

Included within the Port-A-Fort are tires which allow you to jump to the top of the fort from the inside with ease. In addition to offering protection, the top of a fort provides an ideal vantage point for shooting enemies in any direction.

Don't forget, anytime you find tires on the island, jump onto them and you'll bounce up higher than you can jump yourself.

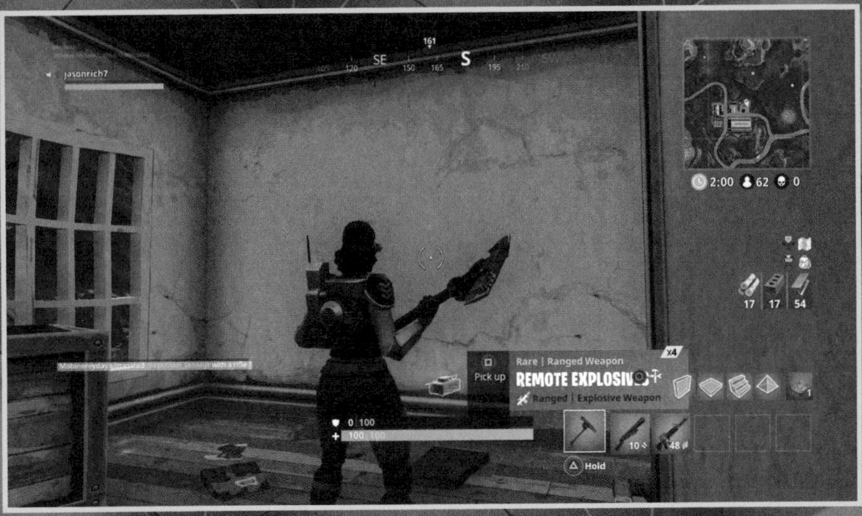

Remote Explosives—A soldier can carry up to ten of these explosives at once. Activate it one by attaching it to an object, wall, or structure, and then detonate it remotely from any distance away. After setting up a remote explosive (shown on the previous page), lure your adversary to its location before detonating it. Just make sure you're far enough away to avoid the explosion yourself.

Shield Potions—Each time you drink a Shield Potion, your shield meter increases by fifty (out of one hundred). Drink two in a row to fully activate and replenish your soldier's shields. This item takes several seconds to consume, during which time your soldier is vulnerable to attack.

Slurp Juice—As you drink this item, your HP and shield strength increases by one point every second (for up to 25 seconds). While you're drinking, your soldier must be standing still and is vulnerable to attack.

Traps—Set a Trap on any structure's floor, wall, or ceiling and then leave it. When an opponent accidently activates the hidden Trap, they'll receive mega-damage. Just make sure you don't set off the Trap yourself once you've activated it, or you'll be the one getting hurt! Shown on the left is a Trap waiting to be picked up and placed into the soldier's backpack for later use.

On the right is what a Trap looks like once it's been place on a wall and activated. Typically, you'd place them where an enemy wouldn't see them.

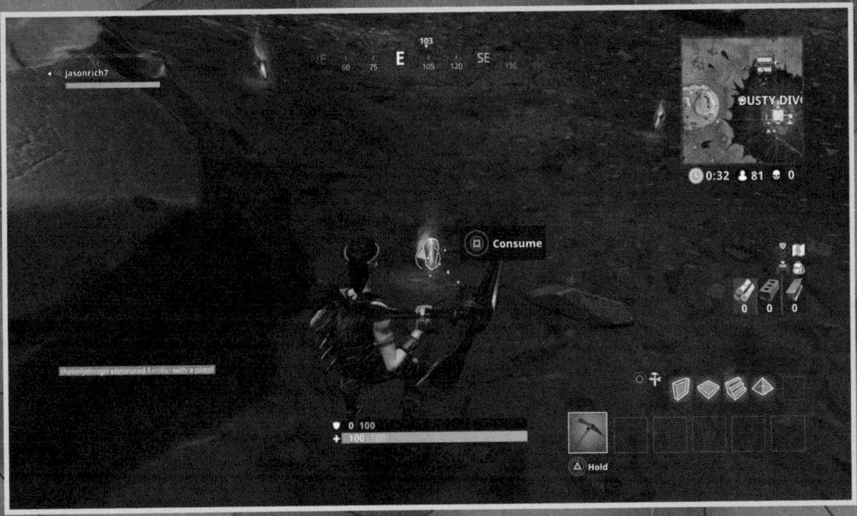

Anytime you explore a crater (at least during Season 4), chances are you'll find **Hop Rocks**. Consume one or more of these rocks, and for a short time, you will be able to jump higher and leap farther. You'll also be protected from harm as a result of a fall.

Clingers look like toilet plungers. Throw them at any object or enemy, and it'll attach. Within a few seconds, BOOM!

Once a Clinger is tossed and attaches to something (in this case a tree), it'll turn blue when activated. It then creates a decent explosion that'll destroy anything in the vicinity and damage (or defeat) enemies.

SECTION 6

WHAT YOU NEED TO KNOW TO BECOME A PRO

Any expert Fortnite player needs to focus on five areas when it comes to fine-tuning their gaming skills. These include:

1. **Exploitation**—Understand the map, where things are, and how to use the different types of terrain to your advantage.
2. **Fighting**—Know how to collect weapons and tools and then choose which one to use based on the enemy soldier(s) you're encountering at any given moment during a match.
3. **Building—**Be able to determine when and where you need to build; what material (wood, stone, or metal) to use; and how to best utilize the structures you build for protection, to increase your visibility, to get yourself higher than your current opponent, or to help you reach an otherwise inaccessible area.
4. **Staying Alive—**Knowing when to fight and when to run or hide, will help keep you alive longer during a match. Based on the tools at your disposal, learn how to hide and then surprise and ambush your enemies, or utilize Traps or Remote Explosives).
5. **Avoiding the Storm—**If you fail to pay attention to the storm, you could easily wind up stuck deep in it, and unable to escape before your HP and shields are depleted. If you must enter into the storm, be sure your HP and Shield Meter are fully charged. Drink a Chug Jug, if possible. This will give you extra time to escape the clutches of the storm.

Know Your Soldier's Capabilities

Knowing how to control your soldier is essential. The more time you in invest playing Fortnite: Battle Royale, the better your muscle memory will become, allowing you to access the appropriate gaming controls quickly and accurately, without having to think too much about it.

The controls used to handle each of a soldier's movements or capabilities vary based on which gaming platform you're using and how you customize the controls.

From the moment your soldier steps foot on the island, he/she has the ability to:

- **Aim and Shoot a Weapon**—A soldier can aim and shoot a weapon while standing still, crouching down, walking, running, or jumping. It's all about timing and aim.
- **Build**—Enter building mode to create or edit walls, stairs/ramps, or fortresses. Remember, you can't build and use weapons at the same time, so you need to practice quickly switching between combat mode and building mode.
- **Crouch**—Get down on your knees to improve your aim when firing a weapon, to hide behind an object or structure, or to make yourself shorter in order to pass under an object (such as a partially open garage door).
- **Dance**—After a victory, or anytime it's safe, showcase some dance moves. If you see someone dancing during a match, proceed with caution. The enemy could be trying to lure you into a trap or ambush. Access the Emote menu to choose your action, after customizing the options from the Locker Screen before a match.
- **Grab Items**—When you see any item (a weapon, ammo, or loot) on the ground, walk up to it and grab it, assuming you have space in your backpack. If there's no space remaining, you can swap between the item on the ground and the one you're currently holding.

- **Jump**—Leap upwards. Use this to avoid an attack, or to quickly climb onto or over an object.
- **Open Chests or Ammo Boxes**—Walk up to a chest or ammo box and press the appropriate controller/keyboard button to open it. Its contents will spread out on the ground. Pick and choose which items you want to pick up. It may be necessary to swap out items in your backpack to accommodate new or more powerful weapons and loot. In some cases, you'll be required to crouch down in order to open a chest or ammo box, depending on its position.
- **Open/Close Doors**—Instead of smashing through a door, you can open and close it. However, anyone who's around will hear the sound of the door's movement. When you walk up to a door, press the appropriate controller/keyboard button when you see an Open or Close message on the screen.
- **Run**—Travel faster than walking. The noise from your soldier's movement will be louder.

- **Share a Graphic Emote**—Toss a graphic icon into the air or perform a movement (such as a salute or dance). By completing challenges, you're able to collect and use a wide range of different emotes. Customize what your soldier can do from the Locker screen before a match.

- **Slide Down Hills/Cliffs**—Instead of jumping off of a steep hill (which reduces your HP), you can safely slide down many hills and cliffs. You can't slide when jumping off of structures, towers, or buildings. Shields do not protect you against falls.
- **Smashing with the Pickaxe**—Use your soldier's pickaxe to smash and collect resources; to break through roofs, walls, floors, or ceilings; or as a close-range weapon.

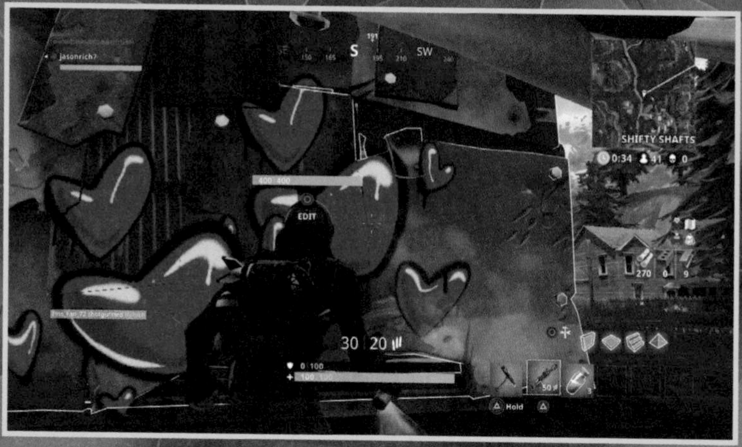

- **Spray Paint a Tag**—This is yet another way your soldier can express him- or herself during a match. This ability can be unlocked by completing challenges (or purchased from the Item Shop). Leave your painted mark on any surface.

An emote, dance, or spray paint tag is done from this Emote menu screen (shown on the previous page) which is accessible anytime during a match.

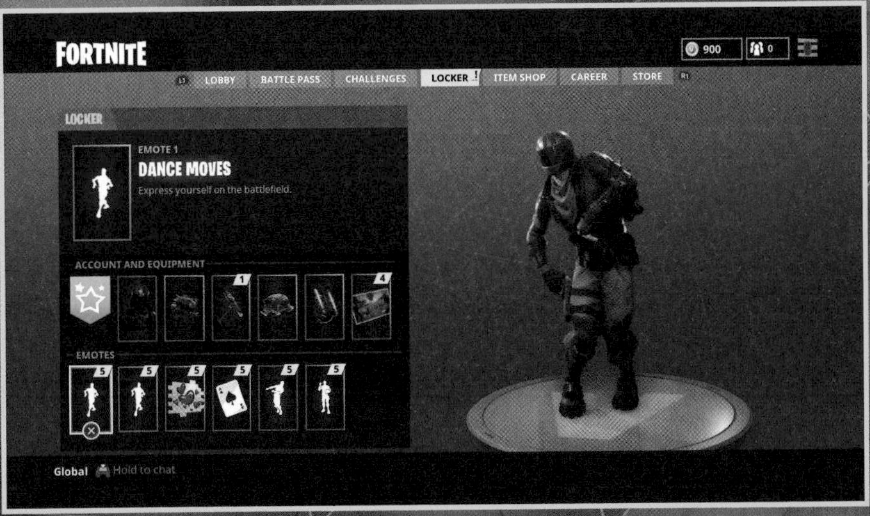

The Emotes menu can be customized before any match by accessing the Locker screen and selecting any of the six Emotes slots. Choose what unlocked content you want to include within each slot. This can include a dance move, graphic, or spray paint tag.

- **Tiptoe**—Crouch down to move slowly and much more quietly.
- **Use Loot**—Knowing when and how to use the loot you've collected can keep you alive longer and help you defeat opponents. Be creative when using Traps, Remote Explosives, and Grenades, for example, and don't waste HP or shield power-ups. As soon as you find a power-up that'll activate your shields, use it. Keep your shields as fully charged as possible throughout a match.
- **Walk**—Move in any direction, at a steady pace. You have full control over the direction your soldier travels. Anytime you move, your soldier's footsteps generate noise.

As for items that will boost your HP, use 'em when you need 'em. Keep in mind that some health and shield power-ups take between five and thirty seconds to consume or utilize, so be sure you're well protected.

Build walls around yourself before drinking a Chug Jug or using a Cozy Firepit, for example, since these take the longest to utilize and leave you exposed. You can't move or do anything else when consuming or using most HP/shield power-ups.

Collect Weapons, Ammo, and Loot from Defeated Soldiers

One of the fastest and easiest ways to build your arsenal and expand your collection of resources during a match is to defeat enemy soldiers and then collect what they leave behind. Just make sure you're well protected when you move in to collect the loot, or another enemy could launch a surprise attack and try to collect what the terminated enemy left behind, as well as what you're carrying if you get defeated as well.

Master the Art of Building

Becoming an expert builder, especially in the heat of battle, requires practice, as well as some creativity when it comes to designing structures. Either by watching livestreams of expert players on YouTube or Twitch.tv, or by staying in Spectator mode after you're eliminated from a match, watch the final stages of matches carefully to learn techniques for building fortresses, and to discover some fort design ideas that work well.

To practice your building technique, travel to an unpopular and unpopulated area of the island, focus on collecting resources, and then fine-tune your building skills. Experiment with different structure designs and develop the skill set needed to be able to build very quickly, without having to think too much about it.

The following are additional strategies to help you become an expert builder:

When building a fortress, cover all sides. Don't forget to build a roof to protect you from assaults from above. Metal is used here, for the first floor of a mini-fortress.

As you're building the foundation of a fort, for example, reinforce the first floor with metal or extra panels. This way, if an enemy manages to sneak up and launch a close-range attack, you'll have extra time to react before your fortress crumbles.

You can use a grenade launcher from a distance to destroy part or all of an enemy fortress, and most types of mid- to long-range shotguns and rifles will also work. However, if you can sneak up on the enemy from the ground, attach a Remote Explosive to the base of their fort, or toss a few grenades. This is typically quicker than continuously shooting at a fortress wall to weaken or destroy it.

In many instances, height is more important than security. Build a quick and tall ramp upwards, and then shoot down at enemies below. Add a vertical wall on both sides of the ramp for added protection. As long as an enemy does not have time to shoot and destroy your ramp while you're at the top of it, you'll be at an advantage. It's safe for your soldier to fall up to three stories when leaping out of a structure you built. If he/she falls from any higher, injury (or worse) will result.

When you need quick protection, build a vertical wall with the strongest material you have available, and then quickly build a ramp (or stairs) directly behind it. You can then crouch down behind this structure for protection. Doing this provides a double layer of shielding that an enemy will have to shoot through or destroy in order to reach you. Plus, by crouching down, you become a smaller target.

Double up on the wall-ramp combo, and then crouch behind it for even greater protection.

In some cases, building two ramps side-by-side gives you an advantage. First, an opponent can't see your exact location when you move back and forth between ramps. Also, if one ramp is about to get destroyed, quickly leap to the other to survive the attack. Yes, this requires more resources, but it's often worth it.

A "ramp rush" is a strategy that involves building a tall ramp quickly, so you're able to move directly toward and over an enemy (or their base) to initiate an attack. Using the double-wide ramp and zigzagging between ramps makes it harder for your enemies to track your exact location.

Smashing wooden pallets (shown on the previous page) often generates more wood than smashing trees. However, trees provide more wood than the walls, floors, and ceilings of houses or buildings. Giant trees, like those found Moisty Mire, tend to generate the most wood. During normal combat, wood is typically the best resource to use. Save your stone and metal for fort building during the final stages of a match.

Harvesting metal from cars and trucks generates the best results, but also creates a ton of noise. Don't forget, when you defeat an enemy, you can collect the weapons and resources (wood, stone, and metal) they leave behind. Defeating two or three enemies during a match will typically allow you to collect more than enough resources without having to harvest too much yourself.

Once you've built one or more walls, instead of wasting time editing the wall to add a window, simply enter Building Mode and face the wall. It will become temporarily transparent. You can see out, but the strength of the wall remains intact for your protection.

Each floor of a basic fort can consist of four walls, with a ramp inside used to reach the next level up. By expanding the width of your fort at various levels, you make it harder for enemies to figure out where you're hiding inside. If opponents have forts taller than yours, or are positioned higher than you, don't forget to add a roof, or keep building onto your fort so it becomes taller.

For enhanced shielding and additional protection against snipers, grenades, and other weapons, place the pyramid-shaped roof structures around the upper perimeter of your fortress.

Consider adding Traps and/or Remote Explosives near the bottom of your fortress, in case an enemy tries to sneak inside to attack you while you're hiding on an upper level of your fort. When you place a Trap, drop some loot below it to lure in enemies.

When your enemy is building a fort close to you, use the same material as them to hide the construction noise, and strive to make your fort taller. Remember, the soldier with the height advantage during a firefight often wins.

If you see a weakness in a tall structure, and you know an enemy is at or near the top of it, shoot at that weak point. Making the structure collapse will cause your enemy to fall. A short fall will have little impact, but a fall from five or more levels up could be devastating.

Learn to Quickly Build "1x1" Fortresses

A 1x1 fortress is simply four walls around you, with a ramp in the center that goes up multiple levels. Using wood allows you to build with the greatest speed, but using metal offers the greatest protection. Keep practicing until you're able to build this type of fortress very quickly, without having to think too much about it.

Here's how to build a 1x1 fortress:

First build four vertical walls so they surround you.

In the center, build a ramp. As the ramp is being constructed (shown on the previous page), jump on it. Keep repeating this process to add levels to your fort.

At the top, consider adding four pyramid-shaped roof pieces around the roof for added protection when you peek out. However, if you need protection from above as well, add a flat roof or a pyramid-shaped roof piece directly over your head.

SECTION 7

PREPARE FOR THE FINAL BATTLES

Those final minutes of a match (known as the "End Game")—when the circle becomes very small and only a few of the most highly skilled enemy soldiers remain alive—are when you'll need to step up and showcase your survival, building, and fightings kills—often at the same time—in order to win the match and become the last person standing.

Step one is to be prepared. Go into the final circle with your HP and Shield Meters fully charged. Plus, have plenty of resources on hand (at least 1,000 to 1,500 wood, stone, and/or metal is ideal). It's also necessary to have the right assortment of weapons in your arsenal. A grenade launcher and/or rocket launcher and a sniper rifle (or rifle with a scope) are definitely must-have weapons.

Never lose sight of your ultimate objective—to be the last person standing at the end of a match.

12 End Game Strategies to Help You Prepare to Win Any Match

Preparation is the key when you enter into the End Game in hopes of winning a match. It's also important to stay calm, watch what your enemies are doing, and stay focused on your objectives.

Here are twelve End Game strategies to help you win:

1. Choose the best location to build your fortress, from which you'll make your final stand in battle. If you're in a good position, you can be more aggressive with your attacks. However, if you're in the dead center of the final circle, you will become the center of attention, which probably isn't good.
2. Make sure your fortress is tall, well-fortified, and that it offers an excellent 360-degree view of the surrounding area from the top level.
3. If your fortress gets destroyed, be prepared to move quickly, and have a backup strategy in place that will help to insure your survival. Having the element of surprise for your attacks gives you a tactical advantage. Don't become an easy target to hit. Keep moving around your fort, or while you're out in the open!
4. During the End Game, don't engage every remaining player. Allow them to fight among themselves to reduce their numbers, and to reduce or even deplete their ammo and resources.
5. Only rely on a sniper rifle (or scoped rifle) to make long-range shots if you have really good aim. Otherwise use explosive weapons that'll cause damage over a wide area, such as a Grenade Launcher or Rocket Launcher.
6. Always keep tabs on the location of your remaining enemies during the End Game. Don't allow them to sneak up behind you. Even if your back is to the storm, an enemy could enter the storm temporarily, and then emerge behind you to launch a surprise attack if you lose track of

their location. Gamers who use the storm to their tactical advantage are referred to as "storm riders." If you lose track of an enemy whom you know is nearby, listen carefully for their movement.

7. Don't invest a lot of resources in a massive and highly fortified fortress until you know you're in the final circle during a match. Refer to the map and the displayed timer. Otherwise, when the storm expands and moves, you could find it necessary to abandon your fort, and then need to build another one quickly, in a not-so-ideal location. Having to rebuild will use up your resources.
8. Base pushers are enemies who aren't afraid to leave their fortress and attempt to attack yours during the final minutes of a match. Be prepared to deal with their close-range threat.
9. If two or three enemies remain, focus on one at a time. Determine who appears to be the most immanent and greatest threat. Be prepared to change priorities at a moment's notice based on the actions of your enemies.
10. Some final battles take place on ramps, not from within fortresses. In this situation, speed, quick reflexes, getting higher up than your enemy, and good aim with the proper weapon are the keys to winning.
11. Have a Chug Jug on hand to replenish your HP and shields if you're attacked, and incur damage, but are not defeated. Make sure you're well protected when you drink the Chug Jug. Med Kits are also great for maintaining HP during End Games.
12. Study the live streams created by expert Fortnite players (on YouTube and Twitch.tv) to learn their End Game strategies, and see how they react to various challenges.

SECTION 8

FORTNITE RESOURCES

Pro gamers around the world have created YouTube channels, online forums, and blogs focused exclusively on Fortnite: Battle Royale. Plus, you can watch pro players compete online and describe their best strategies or check out the coverage of Fortnite: Battle Royale published by leading gaming websites and magazines.

On YouTube (www.youtube.com) or Twitch.TV (www.twitch.tv/directory/game/Fortnite), in the Search field, enter the search phrase "Fortnite: Battle Royale" to discover many game-related channels, live streams, and pre-recorded videos.

Be sure to check out these awesome online resources that will help you become a better Fortnite: Battle Royale player:

WEBSITE OR YOUTUBE CHANNEL NAME	DESCRIPTION	URL
Epic Games' Fortnite YouTube Channel	The official Fortnight YouTube channel.	www.youtube.com/user/epicfortnite
Epic Games' official Fortnite website	Learn all about Fortnite: Battle Royale, as well as the paid editions of Fortnite.	www.Fortnite.com
Epic Games' official Twitter feed for Fortnite	The official Fortnite Twitter feed.	https://twitter.com/fortnitegame (@fortnitegame)
FantasticalGamer	A popular YouTuber who publishes Fortnite tutorial videos.	www.youtube.com/user/FantasticalGamer
Fandom's Fortnite Wiki	Discover the latest news and strategies related to Fortnite.	http://fortnite.wikia.com/wiki/Fortnite_Wiki

FBR Insider	The Fortnite: Battle Royale Insider website offers game-related news, tips, and strategy videos.	www.fortniteinsider.com
Game Informer Magazine's Fortnite Coverage	Discover articles, reviews, and news about Fortnite published by *Game Informer* magazine.	www.gameinformer.com/search/searchresults.aspx?q=Fortnite
Game Skinny Online Guides	A collection of topic-specific strategy guides related to Fortnite.	www.gameskinny.com/tag/fortnite-guides/
IGN Entertainment's Fortnite Coverage	Check out all IGN's past and current coverage of Fortnite.	www.ign.com/wikis/fortnite
Jason R. Rich's Website and Social Media Feeds	Share your Fortnite gameplay strategies with this book's author and learn about his other books.	www.JasonRich.com Twitter: @JasonRich7 Instagram: @JasonRich7
Microsoft's Xbox One Fortnite Website	Learn about and acquire Fortnite: Battle Royale if you're an Xbox One gamer.	www.microsoft.com/en-US/store/p/Fortnite-Battle-Royalee/BT5P2X999VH2
MonsterDface YouTube and Twitch.tv Channels	Watch video tutorials and live game streams from an exert Fortnite player.	www.youtube.com/user/MonsterdfaceLive www.Twitch.tv/MonsterDface
Nomxs	A YouTube and Twitch TV channel hosted by online personality Simon Britton (Nomxs). It features Fortnite game streams.	https://youtu.be/np-8cmsUZmc or www.twitch.tv/videos/259245155
Sony's PS4 Fortnite Website	Learn about and acquire Fortnite if you're a PS4 gamer.	www.playstation.com/en-us/games/fortnite-ps4
Turtle Beach Corp.	This is one of several companies that make awesome quality gaming headsets that work great with a PS4, Xbox One, PC, or Mac. Being able to hear crystal-clear sound and hold conversations with fellow gamers, is essential when playing Fortnite.	www.turtlebeach.com

Your Fortnite Adventure Continues . . .

Epic Games continues to update Fortnite: Battle Royale by making sometimes dramatic alterations to the island map; by introducing challenging new gameplay modes; by revealing exciting new storylines and subplots; by adding powerful new weapons and innovative types of new loot; and by making available eye-catching ways to showcase your soldier's appearance (with outfits, back bling, pickaxes, gliders, emotes, and other customizable elements).

This game continues to evolve, ensuring that it never becomes boring, predictable, or easy to master. Even if you do get really good playing in Solo mode, when you gather one or more friends to compete with you in the Duos or Squads gameplay modes (accessible from the Lobby), the challenges and unpredictability within the game increase dramatically. Teamwork (including constant communication with your allies) becomes important.

Now that you've discovered tons of useful strategies to follow, what will make you a truly awesome gamer is a ton of practice!

Good luck, and more importantly, have fun!